Acclaim for A Ho...

The practice of making a pilgrimage to Rome has always held a place of special significance in the Church's celebration of a Holy Year. By means of her comprehensive guide to celebrating the Jubilee of Mercy in Rome, Joan Lewis provides each pilgrim with thoughtful insights and practical details that are essential for a fruitful pilgrimage to the Eternal City. Every page gives evidence to her great love for Rome and her fervent desire that each sojourner should experience the Jubilee not as a mere tourist but, most of all, as a pilgrim ready to be a witness to the great mercy of God.

— Archbishop Rino Fisichella, President of the Pontifical Council for the Promotion of the New Evangelization

Leave it to Joan to make us feel at home in Rome! For those of you able to accept the invitation of Pope Francis to come as pilgrims to the city of Peter and Paul, make sure you bring Joan's book with you!

— Cardinal Timothy Dolan, Archbishop of New York

Few people have spent as much time as has Joan Lewis in reporting from Rome. In *A Holy Year in Rome* she applies her formidable writing skills, her impressive knowledge of the Eternal City, and her love of our Catholic Faith. Anyone visiting Rome during this year of grace needs to have with them Joan's book in order to make the most of the time. Thank you, Joan, for making Rome all the more accessible to all of us, first-time visitors as well as those who have enjoyed the city for decades.

— Cardinal Donald Wuerl, Archbishop of Washington

I have been going to Joan Lewis for at least thirty-five years for practical guidance around Rome, and what she is hearing on the streets and from her many contacts in every sort of Vatican office. Readers will be delighted by her newest guide to this city, through which thousands will be in touch with what her many friends have been learning from her for years. Joan is an invaluable guide for two reasons: first, she loves Rome, and as an American has been soaking up its daily joys for more than three decades. Second, she loves those who ask guidance from her and presents Rome in an informal, personal, and friendly way, like a companion walking at your side. Enjoy!

—Michael Novak, Witness to Vatican II
and author of *The Open Church* (1964)

Remarkable! In fact, extraordinary! The treasures in this book are as immeasurable as those found in the quaint streets, famous churches, and charming people of Rome! If you've been to Rome and the Vatican, *A Holy Year in Rome* will make you yearn to go back *tomorrow* with a deep newfound knowledge. If you have yet to visit the Eternal City, don't worry—through beautiful descriptive explanations, Joan Lewis makes the city come alive. I felt as though I had not only the best personal tour guide on this spiritual pilgrimage but also a friend by my side, proud to show me the riches of the enchanted city she calls home. Definitely a must read for anyone planning a pilgrimage to Rome (even if it is not during the extraordinary Holy Year)!

—Kelly Wahlquist, Founder of *WINE: Women
In the New Evangelization* and author of *Created
to Relate: God's Design for Peace and Joy*

The book we have been waiting for! A labor of love by Rome expert Joan Lewis, who has for decades lived and breathed the Eternal City. These pages exude Joan's signature warmth as she enchants us with luscious descriptions and immeasurable insights, sharing the real meaning of pilgrimage in her fascinating one-of-a-kind pilgrim's guide to the Holy Year in Rome. I highly recommend this book!

— Donna-Marie Cooper O'Boyle, EWTN TV host,
speaker, and best-selling author of
twenty books, including *The Kiss of Jesus*

There is a good reason why Joan Lewis is one of the most popular and well-received regular contributors to my radio program. Simply put, no one knows Rome quite like Joan. Her book *A Holy Year in Rome* is another great example of her knowledge and love of the Eternal City and, more importantly, her knowledge and love of all things Catholic. *A Holy Year in Rome* is the perfect gift for anyone who desires to learn more about the Church and the place it calls home. It sounds cliché, but thanks to the beautifully detailed descriptions, explanations, and summaries of the different sights, sounds, and sacred places, combined with Joan's extensive knowledge and insider's tips, *A Holy Year in Rome* is, as that old commercial reminds us, the next-best thing to being there.

— Teresa Tomeo, Media expert, motivational speaker,
best-selling author, syndicated Catholic talk-show host
of *Catholic Connection* and *The Catholic View for Women*

There is no better guide to Pope Francis's Rome in the Holy Year of Mercy than Joan Lewis. She is, although young at heart, a living witness of Church history and the uncrowned Queen of the

Vaticanisti, the Vatican-based journalists. More than that, she is a living encyclopedia. Whatever you've always wanted to learn about Rome, the Vatican, the Pope, and the most inner secrets of the Church, Joan knows it all. Nobody could have written a better guide to the Eternal City. She shares her rich insight and knowledge with us in this breathtaking, deeply profound, and always reliable book, which invites us to follow the Pope's invitation, to become pilgrims and to experience the beauty of Rome and the tenderness of God in the Year of Mercy!

— Michael Hesemann, co-author of *My Brother, the Pope*

Distinguished by her longstanding love of all things Roman, as well as her deep understanding of the Church and its rich history, Joan Lewis is the ideal guide for any English-speaking pilgrim to the Eternal City seeking to enter more deeply into the Year of Mercy. No one knows Rome better. I am thrilled that *A Holy Year in Rome* makes it possible for all of us to benefit from her spiritual and practical insights.

— Bernie Hebda, Coadjutor Bishop of Newark

A HOLY YEAR
IN ROME

Joan Lewis

A HOLY YEAR IN ROME

—— ❖ ——

The Complete Pilgrim's Guide
for the Jubilee of Mercy

SOPHIA INSTITUTE PRESS
Manchester, New Hampshire

Sophia Institute Press
Box 5284, Manchester, NH 03108
1-800-888-9344

www.SophiaInstitute.com

Sophia Institute Press® is a registered trademark of Sophia Institute.

Library of Congress Cataloging-in-Publication Data
Names: Lewis, Joan (Rome Bureau Chief for EWTN) author.
Title: A holy year in Rome : the complete pilgrim's guide for the Jubilee of
    Mercy / Joan Lewis.
Description: Manchester, New Hampshire : Sophia Institute Press, 2016. |
    Includes bibliographical references.
Identifiers: LCCN 2015042734 | ISBN 9781622823338 (pbk. : alk. paper)
Subjects: LCSH: Christian pilgrims and pilgrimages—Rome—Guidebooks. | Holy
    Year. | Basilicas—Italy—Rome—Guidebooks. | Christian
    shrines—Italy—Rome—Guidebooks. | Rome (Italy)—Buildings, structures,
    etc.—Guidebooks. | Rome (Italy)—Description and travel.
Classification: LCC BX2320.5.I8 L49 2016 | DDC 263/.0424563—dc23 LC record
available at http://lccn.loc.gov/2015042734

First printing

THE QUALITY OF MERCY

The quality of mercy is not strained.
It droppeth as the gentle rain from heaven
Upon the place beneath. It is twice blessed:
It blesseth him that gives and him that takes.
'Tis mightiest in the mightiest. It becomes
The thronèd monarch better than his crown.
His scepter shows the force of temporal power,
The attribute to awe and majesty
Wherein doth sit the dread and fear of kings,
But mercy is above this sceptered sway.
It is enthronèd in the hearts of kings.
It is an attribute to God himself.
And earthly power doth then show likest God's
When mercy seasons justice. Therefore, Jew,
Though justice be thy plea, consider this,
That in the course of justice none of us
Should see salvation. We do pray for mercy,
And that same prayer doth teach us all to render
The deeds of mercy. I have spoke thus much
To mitigate the justice of thy plea,
Which if thou follow, this strict court of Venice
Must needs give sentence 'gainst the merchant there.

— WILLIAM SHAKESPEARE,
The Merchant of Venice

CONTENTS

Foreword: Finding Mercy in Rome, by Bishop
Robert J. Baker ix

Preface: A Letter from Rome xiii

I. A Journey of the Spirit 3

II. Glossary of Terms 7

III. Jubilees in History 27

IV. A Papal Surprise—a Jubilee Year of Mercy 53

V. The Seven Pilgrimage Basilicas of Rome 69

VI. The Catacombs 131

VII. Vatican City State 141

VIII. Castelgandolfo: History, Beauty, and Peace Make
It a Home for Popes 149

IX. And If You have Time 159

X. Jubilee of Mercy Calendar of Events 169

XI. Joan's Rome: Travel Advice 183

XII. Santa Susanna, the American and
English-Speaking Catholic Community in Rome . . . 195

XIII. Odds and Ends: Miscellaneous Tips for Tourists . . . 201

Bibliography 207

About the Author: Joan Lewis 211

Foreword

FINDING MERCY IN ROME

❖

A pilgrim's journey to Rome can literally change one's life!

From my own days of study in Rome in the 1970s and during my many visits there for retreats and pilgrimages over the years, I have found that Rome and its citizens will embrace you and welcome you, if you allow them that privilege, as the grand colonnade of St. Peter's Square embraces all who enter that great basilica.

No matter how far a pilgrim travels, as he gets close to Rome, he begins to realize that something significant and important is about to happen to his soul. Young or old, rich or poor, cleric or common laborer, the pilgrim is changed, forever touched by this ancient, yet ever new city.

Joan Lewis's *A Holy Year in Rome* will make your pilgrimage to Rome for the Year of Mercy very special. It will indeed be a "Journey of the Spirit" for you! Joan will help you to embrace Rome this Holy Year, as Rome embraces you.

Having worked in Rome for more than thirty-four years at the Vatican and as Rome correspondent for EWTN, with a special

A HOLY YEAR IN ROME

EWTN feature entitled *Joan's Rome*, Joan knows this city inside out. She has known personally recent popes, who have presided over the Catholic household of faith as Chief Shepherds and Vicars of Christ. She has known Princes of the Church and paupers in the pews. She has interviewed royalty and simple folk. To Joan, one's pedigree really doesn't matter. What matters is the uniqueness that each person possesses as a child of God and as a pilgrim on the journey of faith that is one's everyday life.

In addition to participating in numerous papal liturgies in Rome's major basilicas, Joan has attended Mass in many of the city's nearly five hundred churches. She will guide you around Rome and will explain the meaning of terms, the importance of sites, and the history of events significant to this special year—as only she can.

Most importantly she will help you get a grip on the meaning of mercy, as it applies to you. She will help you appreciate the characteristics of Divine Mercy, God's attitude and action of mercy in your life, so that you may:

- bear well and forgive fellow travelers' annoying habits

- seek pardon for your own annoying habits

- be the most courteous person in any gathering

- assist those on the journey who are slower and less flexible than you

- see not only monuments, churches, and basilicas, but the people who work there, keeping them clean and orderly

- be patient and cooperative with security personnel, knowing that they ensure the safety of all

- find some opportunities to give alms to the less fortunate

- see in the faces of those from other races and nations the image of God

- not only travel and see, but stop and reflect

- let your heart be turned over more to those suffering injustice and systemic poverty

- resolve to live in gratitude rather than according to need-less desire

- say thank you to all who serve in any way

A pilgrimage can change you. Joan Lewis wants this Year of Mercy to be special for you. Enjoy her phenomenal help in your discovery of the meaning of mercy in your pilgrimage to Rome this Holy Year!

+Robert J. Baker
Bishop of Birmingham, Alabama

A LETTER FROM ROME

❖

Dear Friends,

Welcome to Rome! Welcome to the Eternal City, where the churches, piazzas, fountains and *palazzi* are old—but the spirit is young! Welcome to a city whose traffic, irrational parking, and inconsistent store hours can drive you to distraction but whose magic persuades you to come back frequently, perhaps even to stay forever, as I decided to do ever so many years ago.

The bureaucracy can be maddening, and quite often the Italians use their inexplicable knack for finding the longest possible route to accomplishing a task—but that is all part of the fun. Italians have managed for millennia to deal with the idiosyncrasies of life here, described by one writer as "the splendid eternal chaos," by rolling with the punches. In Italian this is called *l'arte di arrangiarsi*, the knack of getting along. If something isn't working, they shrug their shoulders and say, *"Pazienza* [patience]!" And eventually it works!

You will be enchanted by Rome and by the Vatican as millions have been before you. The magic is there—it pulsates, vibrates, and defies description. It is in the history, the art, the majestic basilicas, the elegant bridges, the splendid piazzas, the cobblestone streets, the bubbling fountains, and the symphony of church bells. In fact, I hope you can be in Rome sometime at the stroke of midnight when Holy Saturday becomes Easter Sunday and the bells of Rome's nearly five hundred churches toll to proclaim the Resurrection.

The magic is in the smile of a flower vendor, the rich baritone of a waiter who unexpectedly serenades you, or the exuberance of a child playing with the pigeons in Piazza Navona. It is in the air of a deserted city on a Sunday morning, when the city seems to belong to you alone, or the startling quiet of St. Peter's Square in predawn hours as black-robed *monsignori* hurry along to say Mass. It is in the joy of gathering with friends to dine on some of the most scrumptious cooking this side of paradise.

If you have guessed that I love Rome, you are half right. The truth is that I am in love with Rome.

I have the best of both worlds, as they say, for not only am I blessed to live in the city I love, but I am doubly blessed to have worked for the Church I love, and now to cover that Church. For fifteen years I worked on the editorial staff of the Vatican Information Service (VIS), an office within the Holy See Press Office in Vatican City instituted by St. John Paul II in 1990. And now I am blessed once again to cover the Vatican, the Pope, and all things Catholic for EWTN as the Rome bureau chief. More magic!

In the three-plus decades that I've lived here, I have had the pleasure, the joy, and the privilege of escorting countless relatives and friends around Rome and Vatican City, of sharing the history and art, both sacred and profane. My joy is always compounded when I see them fall in love as I did.

The scope of this book is to try to share with you some of the immeasurable treasures of Rome and the Vatican as both prepare to celebrate an extraordinary Holy Year, the Jubilee Year of Mercy proclaimed by Pope Francis in March 2015.

When I wrote a book for the Jubilee Year 2000, a friend pointed out a rather awesome fact about the new millennium as we approached it. Think, he said, of the billions of people who have lived on earth since the start of time. Think of the billions who have lived at the start of a new century. But only a handful, relatively speaking, of all mankind has ever participated in the dawn of a new millennium. Gives one pause for thought!

And that statement is also fairly true of a Jubilee, a Holy Year. There have been very few Jubilees, as you will see in the chapter I dedicate to the history of Jubilees, so we are once again privileged to be among those relatively few who celebrate this special occasion.

Rome and the Vatican have been preparing night and day to see that all will be ready when the celebrations start for the Year of Mercy on December 8, 2015, when Pope Francis opens the Holy Door of St. Peter's Basilica.

The city has been a bit more topsy-turvy than usual since the March 13, 2015, announcement of this special Jubilee. As I write, acres of scaffolding cover buildings as centuries of dirt and grime are removed and many churches, monuments, piazzas, and bridges receive facelifts. For the Jubilee Year 2000, Fiumicino Airport and Termini, the main rail station, underwent vast remodeling and modernization, new buses were ordered, underground parking sites built, roads widened, and underground tunnels constructed to alleviate some of the traffic flow in crucial areas. Pedestrian islands were created, and public park space ("green areas") were enlarged. Additional reception areas and information centers were created. Many similar projects are under way for the current Jubilee.

A HOLY YEAR IN ROME

Although I have lived here for over three decades, in many ways I am still a tourist, still a pilgrim, as I am forever discovering something new—thanks to my many friends who are the true experts, who know far more than I do about history, art, and architecture.

It is not my intention in this book to give you a comprehensive tour of Rome. You will be guided by experts to the Roman Forum and countless other sites. What I hope to share with you is the meaning of a pilgrimage, the significance of the Jubilee, the Holy Year. I'll take you back in time for a look at the history of Jubilees and then bring you to the present with a visit to the seven pilgrim basilicas of Rome, four of which must be visited by pilgrims to obtain a Holy Year indulgence: St. Peter, St. John Lateran, St. Mary Major, and St. Paul Outside-the-Walls.

You ask: What is a Jubilee? What is a basilica? What does "Bull of Indiction" mean? What is an indulgence? Well, I start our tour with a glossary of terms that I hope will make your trip much more meaningful.

You will also have practical questions: When are the Vatican Museums open? How do I get to St. Peter's dome? How do I visit the *scavi*, the pre-Constantine necropolis beneath St. Peter's? Any tips on eating? Tips on giving tips? I've tried to answer these and many other questions in the chapter "Joan's Rome: Travel Advice." At the very end of the book, I offer "Odds and Ends: Miscellaneous Tips for Tourists."

I would love to be your personal guide on your visit to Rome and the Vatican, to accompany you to the myriad and marvelous basilicas, to escort you through the peace and beauty of Vatican City, to watch your expression of awe when you visit the *scavi* beneath St. Peter's, or to share some exquisite pasta with you.

But that is not possible, so my hope is that this book will take my place, that I'll be your companion guide.

A Letter from Rome

I once saw an advertisement for an international hotel chain that said: "Insight into a city takes decades to acquire and just a moment to share." I hope my insights will provide you with a small taste of what I have come to know and love in my years here. Maybe we will even meet, and I can learn from your insights.

Before I close, I want to express heartfelt love and gratitude to so many people, too numerous to list by name.

First and foremost, my family, especially my parents, whose love was so great that they knew how to let go years ago when I wanted to try my wings in a new land, far from home and far from the joy, laughter, and closeness of our family. Both Mom and Dad are looking down on me now and inspiring me as I write.

I thank my friends, near and far, who have always believed in me and enthusiastically cheered me on for whatever project I tackled. I thank my colleagues at EWTN, those in Alabama and those in Rome, for their faith and support. As I thank each and every one of my friends in Rome, at the Vatican and at Santa Susanna's, the church for Americans here in Rome that has been my spiritual home for my entire life in the city. I see your names and faces and smiles, dear friends, and embrace you with much love and gratitude.

To each and every one of you — and to each person reading this book — God sit on your shoulder!

Joan Lewis

A HOLY YEAR
IN ROME

Chapter I

A JOURNEY OF THE SPIRIT

---◆---

Our earthly existence as the People of God is an eschatological journey toward the heavenly Kingdom, our ultimate destination. This divine goal, our raison d'être, too often takes on a secondary importance, however, as we set our eyes on other, more earthly goals, such as careers, homes, and material possessions.

Yet, deep inside each of us, there is an inner yearning to be free of these encumbrances, to know the truth, unfettered by human things. A yearning to know who God is, to understand His goodness, His love for us, His desire for us to be with Him in eternity. A yearning to understand how the saints reached the goal we all aspire to. A yearning to understand how truly unimportant everything else is, if it does not lead us to God.

From Moses in the desert to modern times, man has sought this truth, has sought an understanding of himself, and of God, through pilgrimages. A pilgrimage is not only a trip *to* a destination; it is, as St. Benedict said in his Rule, a *return* to the promised land, to paradise lost, to a place where man can speak to God, one on one. By visiting shrines — be it to seek spiritual benefit, to venerate a sacred object or image, or simply to be in the presence of a holy person — pilgrims take an important step on this road to self-knowledge, and eventually to eternity.

The first disciples were entrusted by Christ with the mission of bringing the Good News "out of their Father's house" and to the four corners of the earth. Since then, pilgrimages have become an inversion of that mission as the faithful seek the route that brings them back to their Father's house.

Pilgrimages, and the role of shrines in the lives of the faithful are, in fact, so important that we find five canons dedicated to this subject in the 1983 *Code of Canon Law*, in the section governing Sacred Places and Times.

Canon 1230 tells us: "The term *shrine* signifies a church or other sacred place to which the faithful make pilgrimages for a particular pious reason with the approval of the local ordinary." Canon 1231: "For a shrine to be called national, the conference of bishops must approve; for it to be called an international one, the Holy See must approve."

The last one, Canon 1234, paragraph 1, states: "At shrines, abundant means of salvation are to be provided the faithful; the word of God is to be carefully proclaimed; liturgical life is to be appropriately fostered, especially through the celebration of the Eucharist and Penance; and approved forms of piety are to be cultivated."

Pope John Paul II, in a homily at the Basilica of Our Lady of Zapopan, Mexico, in 1979, called shrines "places of grace ... places of conversion, penance and reconciliation with God" and "privileged places to encounter an ever more purified faith, which leads to God."

In 1992 in Rome, the Holy Father addressed participants in the First World Congress of the Pastoral Ministry of Shrines and

Pilgrimages and spoke of the aim of a pilgrimage: "It is a basic and founding experience of the believer's state 'homo viator', man *en route* towards the Source of all good and towards his fulfillment. By placing his entire being on this path, his body, his soul and his intelligence, man reveals himself 'in search of God and a pilgrim to Eternity'."

Whatever the reason for an individual's pilgrimage, when it is undertaken with due spiritual preparation, the heart of a shrine becomes enshrined in the heart of the pilgrim. Whether the shrine houses an image of the Virgin Mary or an image, relics, or the remains of a saint, it indelibly becomes part of the pilgrim, with its very special message.

The message, the story, the history varies with each shrine. In some, the story is of conversion. In others, it recounts a life of heroic sacrifice for love of God. And in others, a miracle.

The first "shrine," the shrine par excellence, was Mary, the Mother of God, a "sanctuary" to Jesus for nine months before He began His earthly journey. It is thus no wonder that the overwhelming majority of shrines throughout the world are dedicated to this most perfect of God's creatures, she who succeeded to the highest degree in her encounter with God, in understanding His goodness, His love for us, and His desire that we share the Kingdom of Heaven with Him.

As we start our pilgrimage to the basilica shrines of the Eternal City, we will look at their history, but more important, we will seek to discover why people come back again and again, why they feel compelled to visit a particular place. Are they drawn to Mary? To a saint? To a message?

Often the answer may be found in the votive gifts left at a shrine *per grazie ricevute* (PGR), "for favors received." While you will note a number of these votive offerings at the major basilicas you will visit on your Roman pilgrimage, they are far more numerous at some of Italy's other shrine-basilicas, such as St. Anthony of Padua, St. Francis of Assisi, Our Lady of the Rosary of Pompeii, and the Holy House of Loreto, to name but a few. At these shrines the votive gifts often cover all available wall space and, occasionally, separate rooms are set aside for the pilgrim's thank-yous.

Only the imagination limits the form a votive offering can take. They can range from the standard silver wall plaque engraved with *PGR* to clothing, bicycles from champion racers, canes, crutches, embroidered items, statues, vases, jewelry, baby clothes, military uniforms, awards, diplomas, trophies, model cars, and sports teams' uniforms. And it is up to the imagination to guess the nature of the favor received.

There is even a canon on this subject. Canon 1234, paragraph 2: "Votive gifts of popular art and piety are to be displayed in shrines or adjacent places and kept secure."

So, pack a mental suitcase (don't forget your rosary!) as we start our pilgrimage, traveling not just as tourists, but as Christians seeking that deeper meaning of our life here on earth, undertaking a trip that is not *to* a place, but rather one that is a *return home*.

Chapter II

GLOSSARY OF TERMS

Countless times during the decades I have lived in Rome and accompanied relatives and friends on tours of the Eternal City and Vatican City I have been asked to explain the difference between a church and a basilica, to define liturgical customs, or to illustrate architectural features of buildings. As I am not a historian, liturgist, or architect by profession, I found that often I did not have the precise answer—and so I would research it for the next time we would be together or the next time a group of visitors came to town.

I am better informed now, though still by no means an expert. However, I thought that, to help you on your journey to and through the Jubilee, an explanation of certain terms linked to a pilgrimage and the places we will visit in our short time together might be in order. The following list is not exhaustive, but it does, I believe, cover the major points of interest and will, I hope, enhance your trip.

JUBILEE. A biblical term, from the Hebrew word *jobhel*, "ram's horn." This was a period to be observed every fifty years by the

Jews, during which Jewish slaves were freed, lands were restored to original owners, fields left untilled, and agricultural work undone. The jobhel was blown to announce the start of this jubilee year. As described in Leviticus (25:8-55), the jubilee year fell after every seventh sabbatical year, that is, at the end of seven times seven, or forty-nine, years. Verses 10 through 13 tell us:

> And you shall hallow the fiftieth year, and proclaim liberty throughout the land to all its inhabitants; it shall be a jubilee for you, when each of you shall return to his property and each of you shall return to his family. A jubilee shall that fiftieth year be to you; in it you shall neither sow, nor reap what grows of itself, nor gather the grapes from the undressed vines. For it is a jubilee; it shall be holy to you; you shall eat what it yields out of the field. "In this year of jubilee each of you shall return to his property.

The word *liberty* in verse 10 meant a general release and discharge from all debts and bondages, and a reinstating of every man to his former possessions. This jubilee year began on the Day of Atonement, the tenth day of the seventh month of Tishri.

Jubilare is also a Latin term meaning "to shout for joy." In the Catholic Church, Jubilee Years, also called Holy Years, trace their origins to the first Holy Year established by Pope Boniface VIII in 1300. He set them to occur at hundred-year intervals. However in 1343, Pope Clement VI changed that to fifty-year intervals, and in 1470, Paul II decreed that ordinary jubilees would be celebrated every twenty-five years.

The earliest Christians were frequently depicted as a people on pilgrimage, primarily to Jerusalem and to places associated with the life and death of Jesus. When Jerusalem fell to the Arabs in 638 and travel there became dangerous, Christians went to Rome, the "second Jerusalem," where Sts. Peter and Paul were martyred, and to Edessa, Turkey, and Santiago de Compostela, Spain, to the tombs, respectively, of Sts. Thomas and James.

Jubilees are preeminent religious occasions and periods of great grace: times for the forgiveness of sins and punishment due to sin, for reconciliation between man and God and man and man. As St. John Paul II reminded us in his 1994 apostolic letter *Tertio Millennio Adveniente*, jubilees are not celebrated only in Rome: "On these occasions the Church proclaims 'a year of the Lord's favor', and she tries to ensure that all the faithful can benefit from this grace. That is why Jubilees are celebrated not only 'in Urbe' but also 'extra Urbem'."

Quite simply, a jubilee is the celebration of an anniversary, a period of rejoicing. It may mark a wedding or a period of service, such as the jubilee of priestly ordination or consecration to the religious life. A jubilee celebrated by the Universal Church marks an event touching all Christians, as did the Jubilee Year 2000, when we celebrated the two thousandth birthday of Our Savior, Jesus Christ. As will the Jubilee of Mercy!

Jubilees are "ordinary" when they fall within the preset pattern of years, and they are "extraordinary" when proclaimed for some outstanding event, such as the 1983 year called by Pope John Paul II to celebrate the 1950th anniversary of the Redemption. The Great Jubilee of the Year 2000 was the twenty-sixth ordinary jubilee.

People of many faiths undertake pilgrimages to places of special significance for their religion. Muslims, for example, have made pilgrimages for centuries to Mecca, Saudi Arabia, the birthplace of the prophet Mohammed and the spiritual center of Islam. Every true believer is required by Islamic law to travel to Mecca on a hajj, or pilgrimage, once during his life.

ALTAR. An elevated structure at which religious services are performed, or sacrifices are offered. This is where the Eucharistic sacrifice of the Mass takes place. In the Bible, the Hebrew word for *altar* came from the word meaning "to slaughter for sacrifice." The first mention of an altar in the Bible is in Genesis 8:20: "Then Noah built an altar to the LORD, and took of every clean animal and of every clean bird, and offered burnt offerings on the altar." Abraham also built an altar when he was about to sacrifice his son (Gen. 22:9). The Mass must always be offered on an altar or an altar stone, known as an antimension. *Antimension* means "that which replaces the table." Sometimes known as a portable altar, it is a square piece of linen on which is imprinted a representation of the Passion and burial of Christ. Both altar and altar stone must contain a relic or relics and must be consecrated by a bishop, or by one who has been given the faculty to do so.

APSE. The architectural term for the semicircular vaulted area or polygonal recessed area of basilica-style churches. The apse is at the extreme opposite end of the entrance of a church. The main altar is located at the center of the apse and is usually surrounded by seats for the main celebrants of liturgical services.

ATRIUM. In its earliest meaning, *atrium* referred to the vestibule or entry of a Roman or Greek house. Much the same today, it refers to the first or principal entry—internal or external—of a building, usually decorated or flanked by columns. The atrium in St. Peter's, for example, is the broad open area between the façade (the front or face of a building) and the actual entrance of the basilica itself. The plural can be *atria* or *atriums*.

BALDACHIN, BALDACHINO. The canopy or covering over the high altar. Though rarely found in modern churches, a baldachin was used for centuries in major churches and was always found over a papal altar. They were prevalent in the Renaissance.

BASILICA. From the Greek *basilike oikia*, "royal house," where the princely ruler lived, this term in Roman times applied to all official buildings built in a particular style. The term was used for early or medieval Christian churches built in a certain style: a nave, two or four aisles, one or more semicircular vaulted apses, and open timber roofs. Now this is an honorific title given to the most eminent churches.

There are two kinds of basilicas: major and minor. Rome has seven major basilicas: St. Peter's, St. John Lateran, St. Mary Major, St. Paul Outside-the-Walls, St. Lawrence Outside-the-Walls, Holy Cross in Jerusalem, and St. Sebastian. Basilicas usually have special privileges reserved to them, such as the granting of certain indulgences. Not all historians, however, classify St. Lawrence Outside-the-Walls as a major basilica.

The first four of these major basilicas are also called papal basilicas. They were once called patriarchal basilicas until Benedict XVI in 2006 eliminated one of the nine titles of the Roman Pontiff, Patriarch of the West. The word *patriarch* comes from the Greek for "ruler of a family." A patriarch is a bishop who holds the highest rank, after that of Pope, in the hierarchy of jurisdiction. Major patriarchs hold the title or see of one of the five great patriarchates: Rome, Constantinople, Alexandria, Antioch, and Jerusalem.

The four papal basilicas are St. John Lateran, the archbasilica for the patriarch of Rome, St. Peter for the patriarch of Constantinople, St. Paul Outside-the Walls for the patriarch of Alexandria, and St. Mary Major for the patriarch of Antioch. St. Lawrence Outside-the-Walls has been assigned to the patriarchate

A HOLY YEAR IN ROME

of Jerusalem. (The Vatican website uses the word to describe the four major basilicas but not St. Lawrence.)

When Boniface VIII instituted Holy Years, pilgrims had the obligation to visit St. Peter and St. Paul Outside-the-Walls. In 1350 Pope Clement VI added St. John Lateran (this is the Pope's cathedral church as Bishop of Rome). During the 1390 Jubilee Year (called by Urban VI and celebrated by Boniface IX), St. Mary Major became the fourth basilica that the faithful had to visit on pilgrimage to Rome. Three more were added to the itinerary for the 1575 Holy Year—St. Lawrence, St. Sebastian, and Holy Cross in Jerusalem—thus bringing to seven—a number considered sacred—the number of churches that pilgrims had to visit to obtain an indulgence.

BISHOP. From the Greek *episkopos*, meaning "overseer" or "guardian," the bishop is the supreme authority of a diocese. Bishop is the highest of the three levels of holy orders, the other two being deacon and priest. Bishops are successors to the Apostles and are responsible to the Pope, the Bishop of Rome. They are not delegates of the Holy See—they exercise their powers by virtue of their office—but are subject to its authority. Bishops are addressed as "Excellency."

BULL. From the Latin *bulla*, "seal," bulls, or bullas, refer to the lead or wax seal that was formerly affixed to important Church documents. By extension, the word has come to mean the papal or apostolic document itself. A bullarium is a collection of papal bulls.

CARDINAL. Following that of Pope, the title of cardinal is the highest dignity in the Catholic Church and was recognized as early as the pontificate of Sylvester I (314-335). Rooted in the Latin word *cardo*, "hinge," cardinals are created by a decree of the Roman Pontiff and are chosen to serve as his principal collaborators and assistants. Cardinal is an honorific title and not one of the three ordained orders (deacon, priest, and bishop). In the earliest years of the Church, a cardinal could be a layman. Today, however, only bishops are named cardinals (and if not a bishop, a cardinal must be ordained to the episcopacy). Cardinals who work for the Roman Curia and reside either in Vatican City or in Rome are considered citizens of Vatican City. Cardinals are addressed as "Eminence."

Canon 349 of the *Code of Canon Law* states: "The cardinals of the Holy Roman Church constitute a special college whose responsibility is to provide for the election of the Roman Pontiff in accord with the norm of special law; the cardinals assist the Roman Pontiff collegially when they are called together to deal with questions of major importance; they do so individually when they assist the Roman Pontiff especially in the daily care of the universal Church by means of the different offices which they perform."

Since 1059, cardinals have been the exclusive electors of the Pope, the Bishop of Rome. The College of Cardinals was constituted in its present form in 1150: it has a dean, who is the bishop of Ostia (near Rome), and a chamberlain, or *camerlengo*, who administers the patrimony of the Church when the See of Peter is vacant. The number of members varied over the centuries. By the time of Pope Paul V (1555-1559) there were 70 members of the College of Cardinals; that increased to 76 under Pius IV (1559-1565). Today, there are more than double that number, but only 120 members—all under the age of eighty—are allowed to enter into conclave to elect a new Pope. That maximum number of cardinal electors was chosen by Pope Paul VI, who, by the way, in 1965 extended the College of Cardinals to include the oriental patriarchs.

A HOLY YEAR IN ROME

When a Pope chooses those who will become cardinals, he has the option of keeping one or more names *in pectore*, "in the breast." That is to say, he does not publicly reveal the name along with the other cardinals-designate because to do so could be inconvenient or dangerous for the person involved. Often a country's political situation is behind such a decision. For example, Pope John Paul II, in his first consistory to name new cardinals in June 1979, reserved a name *in pectore*. The name was revealed years later, and it turned out to be Cardinal Ignatius Gong Pin-mei of mainland China, who, after more than thirty years in prison, had finally been released. Two more *in pectore* were reserved in February 1998 when John Paul II held his seventh such consistory.

CATACOMBS. According to the Vatican-based Latinitas Foundation, the word *catacomb* is derived from both the Greek *kata* meaning "under," and the Latin *cumba*, meaning "cavity." It referred to a consecrated underground cemetery complex but was more than a traditional burial site because the Eucharist was celebrated there. The word *catacomb* was first used in association with the St. Sebastian Cemetery in Rome and referred to a hollowed-out place. This place name referred to a depressed area on the Old Appian Way between the St. Sebastian Cemetery and the tomb of Cecilia Metella and soon was extended to refer to all ancient underground cemeteries, Christian and Jewish. Since their existence was known to the Roman authorities, catacombs were not used by Christians, as is generally believed, as hiding places during the persecutions in the first centuries after Christ. Some tour guides, however, speak of early Christians hiding in the catacombs.

Essentially the catacombs consist of long galleries, some of which have chambers opening out from them. The terrain was soft enough to allow for the excavation of miles of chambers, yet firm enough to withstand the risk of caving in. Often they were constructed on land donated by wealthy Christians that was outside the city walls, as Roman law forbade the burial of the dead within the city walls. On both sides of a gallery, long niches were carved out to bury the dead, occasionally as many as three layers high, in a shelf-like pattern. It is estimated that there are hundreds of miles of galleries in catacombs in Rome alone.

CATAFALQUE. From the Late Latin word *catafalicum*, for scaffolding or a wooden siege tower, this is an elaborate structure in which the body of a deceased person lies in state. It is also the name for the *castrumdoloris*, the middle of the three coffins in which a deceased Pope is buried.

CATHEDRAL. From the Latin *cathedra*, "chair," this refers to both the chair of the bishop who governs a diocese, and thus symbolizes his teaching authority, and to the church itself in which the bishop celebrates the principal liturgical ceremonies in his diocese. The cathedral church must be within the geographical boundaries of the diocese and is usually in the city in which the bishop exercises his authority. A cathedral church is named for the patron saint of the diocese; if named for another, it is a pro-cathedral.

CIBORIUM. Today this word refers to a vessel, usually metal, in which consecrated hosts, particles of the Blessed Sacrament, or the Sacred Species, are kept for distribution at Communion time. It is kept in the tabernacle of the altar or in a room reserved in a church for the Blessed Sacrament. The plural is *ciboria*.

The word comes from the Greek *kiborion* and originally referred to a canopy of wood, stone, or marble resting on four or more pillars that covered an altar. Today, it is more customary to use the Western term *baldachin* (see above) in describing such a canopy or covering. According to the *Catholic Encyclopedia*, the word *baldachin* comes from *baldacco*, "meaning Baghdad, because many rich fabrics from that city were used in the adornment of these canopies [which], in the Middle Ages, were often suspended from the ceiling or projected from the wall to cover an altar or episcopal throne." In time ciboria or baldachins were mandatory over main altars or where the Blessed Sacrament was housed, but this was discontinued under Pope Paul VI.

ECUMENISM. A term denoting all that promotes or fosters Christian unity throughout the world. Meaning "general" or "universal," it comes from the Greek *oikoumenikos*, "to inhabit." Vatican Council II (1962-1965) expressed its interest in the ecumenical movement in the decree *Unitatis Redintegratio* (The Reestablishment of Unity).

Ecumenism featured prominently in Pope John Paul II's hopes for the Holy Year 2000. In his apostolic letter *Tertio Millennio Adveniente* of November 1994 on that Jubilee Year, he wrote: "Among the most fervent petitions which the Church makes to the Lord [for the Jubilee Year 2000] ... is that unity among all Christians of the various confessions will increase until they reach full communion." He also suggested that "the ecumenical and universal character of the Sacred Jubilee can be fittingly reflected by a meeting of all Christians. This would be an event of great significance."

EVANGELIZATION. From the Greek *euangelion*, meaning "good news" or "gospel." Quite simply, evangelizing is the act of preaching the gospel, or spreading the "good news," and refers to any and all activities through which and by which the Church communicates the saving message of Christ.

Glossary of Terms

HOLY DOOR. This is a walled-up door, actually a double door, found in each of the four major Roman basilicas to be visited by pilgrims during a Holy Year. The cemented or walled-up portion is on the inside of the Church and it is this part that is dismantled to allow the outer door to be opened for a Holy Year.

These doors in the past were generally opened on Christmas Eve preceding the Jubilee Year and closed the following Christmas. The Pontifical Council for Promoting the New Evangelization has set a calendar for the opening of the Holy Doors of the Jubilee of Mercy, and they will be opened on four dates. Pope Martin V introduced the ceremony of opening Holy Doors in 1423 when he opened the first one at St. John Lateran. Pope Alexander VI opened the first Holy Door at St. Peter's (the predecessor to the basilica we see today) in 1499. It was he who instituted the rites for these ceremonies, rites that are still, for the most part, used today.

In St. Peter's, the Holy Door is the last to the right of the five doors in the basilica's atrium, and it is always opened by the Holy Father.

These doors are called Holy Doors not only because of the symbolism—doors opening to allow the faithful physically to enter a Church as well as to enter a year dedicated to sanctifying their soul—but because all of the materials used to build the doors, and the hammers used to open them, are blessed. In the Gospels, Jesus Himself tells us that He is the door to heaven.

Twice in history the privilege of having a Holy Door opened fell to the Church of Santa Maria in Trastevere when it was substituted for St. Paul Outside-the-Walls: in 1625 floods had rendered St. Paul's inaccessible, and in 1825 it was again unavailable due to a fire two years earlier. *Tevere* is the Italian word for the Tiber River; *trastevere* means "across the Tiber."

A HOLY YEAR IN ROME

Holy Doors over the Years: I thought you might enjoy a fascinating Vatican Radio program presented and produced by Veronica Scarisbrick about the opening of Holy Doors for a Jubilee. Her background information and an interview with the late Father John Charles-Roux will elicit both wonder and laughter.

Veronica looks at some of the rituals regarding Jubilee Years over the centuries and shares an eyewitness account of the opening of the Holy Door for the Jubilee of 1950, an occasion during which frenzied crowds came along armed with scissors to snip at the cassock of Pius XII.

Veronica and I have been friends for years and she is the cohost of my Vatican Radio program, *Joan Knows*. With her kind permission, I offer the following:

Once upon a time, the Holy Doors of the major basilicas here in Rome were not as magnificent to look at as they are today. Simplicity was the name of the game, and rather than being elaborate with bronze decorations they were in plain wood and bricked in on both sides. That's to say, from the years 1500 to 1950.

The knocking down of any such door, even after that date, was a worrisome affair, as masons had to make sure rubble did not reach anywhere near those standing by—something not always avoided, or anyway not at Saint Peter's Basilica on Christmas Eve 1964, when cement fragments fell near Blessed Paul VI.

After these masons, or "San Pietrini," as the basilica's masons are known, had accomplished their task, the Pope took a hammer and in a symbolic gesture tapped on the Holy Door and pushed it open. To this day, we have many an example of these hammers, precious objects made of gold, gilded silver, or even ivory.

Point of fact: silver and gold were also used for a couple of the bricks to be symbolically placed within the walls as reported in a Chronicle of the Jubilee Year of 1423: people show such devotion to the bricks and cement fragments that as soon as the door is uncovered they are carried away in a general frenzy.

And it seems at a later date, during the opening of the Holy Door by Pope Pius XII to mark the Holy Year of 1949, this rather surprising frenzy astonished someone who attended this event. He's the late Father John Charles-Roux, who, somewhat horrified, recounts what he himself witnessed on this occasion.

His story begins with the practice of the exchanging of skull caps between the Pope and the people: "In the last years of his reign he used to give his skull cap to people. Yes ... you went to a special shop where they had the exact measurements for the circumference of his head and you bought one there ... the direct result of what I saw happened at the opening of the Holy Door. The people, especially Spaniards and South Americans, used to come with scissors and, when he passed by, tried to cut something off his cassock. Of course, they didn't always get hold of his cassock, so the pope used to come back bleeding."

That's why, says Father Charles-Roux in this archived interview, in an effort to persuade people to put their scissors away, a member of the "*anticamera*" suggested fueling the enthusiasm of those present by encouraging them to take away the Pope's skull cap instead ... a practice already in vogue anyway during the pontificate of Pius X.

Our Rosminian priest's eyewitness account also relates to Pius XII and his papal throne: "At the opening of the Holy Door, his throne covered in white damask was quite decent during the first part of the ceremony, but when we came out of Saint Peter's hardly anything remained of the chair, wood-worms could not have done a better job. The chair had been destroyed."

Getting back to the Holy Doors, as mentioned, there are four of them in Rome, one at each of the major Roman basilicas: St.

A HOLY YEAR IN ROME

John Lateran, St. Mary Major, St. Paul Outside-the-Walls, and, of course, Saint Peter. In Saint Peter's, although the last wooden door was installed during the pontificate of Benedict XIV in 1748, the one we see today was placed there in 1949. It's an elegant bronze door, and I once went there to take a closer look. This is what I saw:

> The panels represent scenes that have as their theme that of every Holy Year. That's to say, reconciliation, reconciliation between God and man. For example, there's the representation of Our Lord telling the Apostles you must forgive your brother seventy times seven, not just seven times. There is the representation of the Crucifixion; here another has the representation of the Resurrection. Pilgrims come here to cross the threshold of St. Peter's and are meant to repent while they do, so they may gain access to grace and reconciliation.
>
> Like most of the doors to the basilica, this bronze one is relatively modern. It was designed during the pontificate of Pius XII, who drew attention to the symbolic significance attached to the Holy Door from a biblical, theological, liturgical, and pastoral point of view in terms of salvation history.

To note: the concept of the Holy Door was introduced only in the year 1500, by Alexander VI, the Borgia Pope.

No doubt, when Pope Francis taps on the Holy Door of Saint Peter's Basilica to mark the beginning of this Extraordinary Holy Year of Mercy, which ends on the Feast of Christ the King in 2016, he may add other elements to the traditional ritual for the Jubilee Year he called, because he feels: "The whole Church—that has much need to receive mercy because we are sinners—will find in this jubilee the joy to rediscover and render fruitful the mercy of

God with which we are called to give consolation to every man and woman."

HOLY SEE. A see, from the Latin *sedes*, meaning "chair," an ancient symbol of authority, refers to the place from which a bishop governs his diocese, that is, a specific geographical territory over which he has the pastoral care of Catholics. The Holy See (sometimes called the Apostolic See) is the see of Peter, that is, of the Bishop of Rome, who is the Pope. *Holy See*, referring to the primacy of the Pope, denotes the moral and spiritual authority exercised by the Pontiff through the central government of the Church, the Roman Curia. Although this government is located in Vatican City, the Holy See is not synonymous with the Vatican.

"Serving the Human Family: The Holy See at the Major United Nations Conferences," a volume published in the spring of 1998 by the Holy See Permanent Observer Mission to the UN, defines the Holy See thus: "Basically the term 'Holy See' refers to the supreme authority of the Church, that is, the Pope as Bishop of Rome and head of the College of Bishops. It is the central government of the Roman Catholic Church. As such, the Holy See is an institution which, under international law and practice, has a legal personality that allows it to enter into treaties as the juridical equivalent of a State, and to send and receive diplomatic representatives."

HOLY YEAR. A Holy Year is a period decreed by the Pope for the universal Church during which the faithful may acquire plenary indulgences by fulfilling certain conditions established by the Church. Each time a Holy Year is proclaimed, the reigning Pontiff specifies the conditions for gaining the plenary indulgence of the Jubilee. These are usually set forth in papal bulls.

A HOLY YEAR IN ROME

INDULGENCE. The *Catechism of the Catholic Church* (no. 1471) defines *indulgence* as "a remission before God of the temporal punishment due to sins whose guilt has already been forgiven, which the faithful Christian who is duly disposed gains under certain prescribed conditions through the action of the Church which, as the minister of redemption, dispenses and applies with authority the treasury of the satisfactions of Christ and the saints."

"An indulgence is either partial or plenary according as it removes either part or all of the temporal punishment due to sin. Indulgences may be applied to the living or dead." Partial indulgences remit a part of the punishment due for sin at any given moment, the proportion of such part being expressed in terms of time (thirty days, one year, et cetera). Plenary indulgences require that one be free of venial sin.

Indulgences attached to objects such as rosaries cease to exist when those objects cease to exit. Indulgences attached to prayers are lost by any addition, omission, or alteration. Those unable to go to Rome during Holy Year may benefit from plenary indulgences in their own dioceses under the same conditions.

INTERRELIGIOUS DIALOGUE. This is the dialogue between Catholicism and Christianity in general, as well as with other religious denominations such as Judaism and Islam.

MARTYROLOGY. Considered a liturgical book, this is a list of all the martyrs and saints whom the Church venerates and celebrates in her liturgies. *Martyr* is from the Greek *martyria* and refers to one who stands steadfast in the Faith, usually to the point of dying for the Catholic Faith, or for any article of the Faith, or to preserve a Christian virtue The first martyrology dates from the fifth century and is named after St. Jerome, *Hieronymian Martyrology.* In the ninth century, short descriptions of the saints' lives were added. A sixteenth-century compendium, composed by the Council of Trent (1545-1563), was called the *Roman Martyrology* and was based on the ninth-century one.

Pope John Paul II had suggested a "new Martyrology" for the Jubilee Year 2000. In *Tertio Millennio Adveniente*, he pointed out that "the witness [of martyrs] must not be forgotten.... In our own century the martyrs have returned, many of them nameless, 'unknown soldiers' as it were, of God's cause. As far as possible their witness should not be lost to the Church. As was recommended in the Consistory [which met to plan the Jubilee Year 2000], the local churches should do everything possible to ensure that the memory of those who have suffered martyrdom should be safeguarded, gathering the necessary information. This gesture cannot fail to have an ecumenical character and expression. Perhaps the most convincing form of ecumenism is the ecumenism of the saints and the martyrs.... It will be the task of the Apostolic See, in preparation for the Year 2000, to update the martyrologies for the universal Church, paying close attention to the holiness of those who in our own time lived fully by the truth of Christ."

And Pope Francis speaks of martyrs, modern martyrs, on frequent occasions, very often at his morning Mass in the Santa Marta residence and almost as often at the Sunday Angelus or Regina Coeli. For example, in his April 21 homily at morning Mass, he called those killed today for their faith modern Stephens because they suffer as the Church's first martyr did. "The Church today is a Church of martyrs: they suffer, they give their lives, and we receive the blessing of God for their witness. In these days how many Stephens there are in the world! Let us think of our brothers whose throats were slit on the beach in Libya; let's think of the young boy who was burned alive by his companions because he was a Christian."

NAVE. From the Middle Latin *navis*, meaning "ship," this is the central longitudinal part of a church that runs from the entrance to the main altar and is usually flanked by one or more aisles. These side aisles are the same length but usually of lesser width.

PENANCE, PENITENT. Penance refers both to the sacrament of Penance (better known as Confession and commonly called the sacrament of Reconciliation), wherein a sinner confesses his sins to a priest, and to the virtue of penance, which enables a person to recognize and admit his faults with contrition and a firm promise of amendment. A penitent is a person who seeks forgiveness and reconciliation with God and the Church.

PILGRIM, PILGRIMAGE. A pilgrim is one who undertakes a pilgrimage, that is, a journey to a sacred place, as an act of religious devotion. It may be to venerate a holy place, a relic, or another object of devotion, to do penance, to offer thanksgiving for a favor or favors received or to ask for such favors, or any combination of these. A pilgrimage is symbolic of our earthly existence, that is, of our journey to the heavenly Kingdom. Pilgrimages may be individual or group undertakings and may be to places close to home or to distant countries. After the eighth century, pilgrimages were often imposed in substitution for public penance. The Old Testament exhorted all to show hospitality to pilgrims (Deut. 14:29; Lev. 23:22).

POPE. The Bishop of Rome, or Roman Pontiff. When, upon the death of a Pope, the College of Cardinals enters into conclave to elect his successor, they elect not the Pope but, rather, the Bishop of Rome, who, by virtue of that office is Pope. Canon 331 of the *Code of Canon Law* states: "The bishop of the Church of Rome, in whom resides the office given in a special way by the Lord to Peter, first of the Apostles and to be transmitted to his successors, is head of the college of bishops, the Vicar of Christ and Pastor of the Universal Church on earth; therefore, in virtue of his office he enjoys supreme, full, immediate and universal ordinary power in the Church, which he can always freely exercise."

PORTICO. From the Latin *porticus*, "porch," this is the outside covered entrance to a building, a walkway composed of a roof supported by columns or pillars.

SHRINE. From the Latin *scrinium*, a box for writing materials, this word is now used to refer to a receptacle for sacred relics, or a reliquary. In its broadest (and most commonly used) sense, it refers to the church or consecrated structure that houses a relic (often the remains of a saint or some part of the saint's body or clothing) or an image dedicated to Our Lord, the Blessed Virgin Mary, or a saint.

TABERNACLE. From the Latin word *tabernaculum*, meaning "tent." The Jewish tabernacle, or "portable temple," was actually more elaborate and splendid than is implied by our notion of the word *tent*. Moses built a Tabernacle according to instructions from God (Exod. 25-27; 36-38; 40). This Tabernacle of the Covenant was intended for consulting God on important matters. It was actually four tents, one on top of the other, with the innermost one of the greatest beauty, enclosed in a court of the dimensions given by God, that is, 100 by 50 cubits (150 by 75 feet). When Solomon built his Temple to replace the Tabernacle, portions of the Tabernacle were kept as mementoes in a room of the Temple.

A tabernacle, as we will see on our visits to the churches, is also a canopied recess or niche, or the canopied covering over a main altar.

Today, however, *tabernacle* principally refers to the adorned receptacle housing the ciborium in which the Blessed Sacrament is reserved in churches, chapels, or oratories. Canon 938 of the 1983 *Code of Canon Law* states: "[Paragraph 2:] The tabernacle in which the Most Holy Eucharist is reserved should be placed in a part of the church that is prominent, conspicuous, beautifully decorated, and suitable for prayer. [Paragraph 3:] The tabernacle in which the Eucharist is regularly reserved is to be immovable, made of solid and opaque material, and locked so that the danger of profanation may be entirely avoided."

TRANSEPT. The major transverse or cross part of the body of a church. The transept crosses the nave (the principal longitudinal part of a church, which runs from the entrance to the farthest part, or apse) at the entrance to the choir and, when extended on either side as an arm, thus gives a church the form of a cross.

TRIUMPHAL ARCH. As an architectural term applied to churches, this is the massive overhead arch that separates the apse and nave of a church. In the early Christian era, this was a symbolic reference to the victory of Christianity over paganism. Later the arches were magnificently decorated, either with stupendous mosaics or painted surfaces, to depict religious themes or tell the story of important events in the Church: the Annunciation; the birth of Christ; Christ's life, death, and Resurrection, and so forth.

Chapter III

JUBILEES IN HISTORY

❖

The very first Holy Year was the Jubilee of the year 1300, called for by Pope Boniface VIII.

We are told that in late December 1299 and early January 1300, huge crowds of Romans flocked to St. Peter's Basilica, having heard rumors that extraordinary indulgences would be obtained by those who prayed at the tomb of the first Pope or who venerated Veronica's veil. This relic, a recent arrival to the basilica and called quite simply "the Veronica"—from *vera* (true) *icona* (icon or image)—was allegedly the veil with which Jesus' face was wiped, leaving a perfect image, as he carried the Cross through Jerusalem to Calvary.

Pilgrimages continued throughout the month of January, with ever-growing numbers of faithful visiting the basilica. Pope Boniface, reading the signs of the times, consulted the cardinals of the Curia, and on February 22, 1300, he promulgated the decree *Antiquorum habet digna fide relatio*, with which he instituted the Jubilee.

According to that decree, those who wished to obtain a plenary indulgence "must visit the basilicas of St. Peter and St. Paul for 30 days continuously, or interpolatedly and at least once a day if they were Romans, or fifteen days in the same manner if they were foreigners." Previously, indulgences had been granted only on exceptional occasions. Thus, with this papal bull, the plenary indulgence became part and parcel of Jubilee celebrations.

History records that the city of Rome made preparations to accept foreign pilgrims worthily, including increasing the number of places one could obtain food and lodging. Another gate was opened in the city walls to receive the influx of visitors and the famous Sant'Angelo Bridge, which crossed the Tiber to the Vatican, was divided into two lanes by a short wall, with arriving pilgrims on one side and departing pilgrims on the other. As "all roads lead to Rome," roads from major cities in Europe were often improved, and bridges were either restored or repaired.

In medieval times, the three most prominent destinations for pilgrims were Rome (to the tombs of Sts. Peter and Paul), Santiago de Compostela in Spain (tomb of St. James), and Jerusalem (the Holy Sepulchre). Pilgrims to Rome were called *romeos*, those to Spain *jacquaires* (from *Jacques*, French for James), and those to Jerusalem *palmieri*, "palm bearers," because, as a symbol of their pilgrimage, they brought home a palm branch from the Holy Land.

Often the pilgrims bore a distinctive mark on their hats or clothing. Visitors returning from Rome had either the image of Sts. Peter and Paul or that of the Holy Face (from Veronica's veil, preserved in St. Peter's Basilica); for Jerusalem pilgrims, the palm was again their symbol, and for those coming from Compostela, it was a scallop shell. A pilgrim's outfit usually consisted of a walking staff, a shoulder bag to carry necessities, a broad hat to protect against sun and rain, and a cape, known as a pelerine (from *peregrinus*, meaning "one who comes from afar"). These capes were frequently impregnated with wax to shield travelers against the rain and the cold.

Jubilees in History

In 1300 Pope Boniface VIII had decreed that future Holy Years would take place at hundred-year intervals. However, in 1343, a delegation of Romans, including members of noble families, went to see Pope Clement VI in Avignon, France, where the seat of the papacy had been moved in 1309. They petitioned the Pope to change the frequency of Holy Years, reasoning that most people would never live long enough to celebrate a Jubilee. Clement responded by calling for a Holy Year in 1350, and he decreed that they be celebrated every fifty years.

The Jubilee of 1350 was indeed celebrated in Rome but without the Pope, as it was not until 1377, during the pontificate of Gregory XI, that the Holy See was transferred back to Rome. It was a difficult Jubilee, as Rome had allowed many buildings and monuments to deteriorate during the Avignon period. Too, the plague had swept Europe in 1348, and, although it spared Rome to a great extent, some pilgrims were still afraid to make a trip to the Eternal City. Romans, however, in thanksgiving to the Virgin for having generally spared them, had erected the famous marble staircase of Ara Coeli, "Altar of Heaven," leading to the church of the same name. In 1349 the city was struck by a violent earthquake that damaged many buildings, including the basilicas of St. Paul, St. Peter, and St. John Lateran, in addition to those that had been neglected during the transfer of the papacy.

Pope Urban VI, successor to Gregory XI, who returned the papacy to Rome from Avignon, decided in 1389 to celebrate that return with a Jubilee. He also decided that henceforth Jubilees would occur every thirty-three years, the age of Jesus at His death. However, this meant that the one after 1350 should have taken place in 1383. As it was now 1389—thus too late—he called for a Jubilee to be held in 1390. Urban VI, however, died before officially opening the Holy Year: this task fell to his successor, Boniface IX.

A HOLY YEAR IN ROME

Boniface celebrated a second Jubilee Year in 1400, following the directives of his namesake predecessor who in 1300 had directed that Holy Years be held at every turn of a century. Historians are not always in agreement on whether to include 1400 as an official Jubilee, given that there was no bull of convocation. It appears that the term *Holy Year* appeared for the first time in 1400, although *Jubilee* continued to be used.

Pope Martin V, following Urban VI's decree of Jubilees at thirty-three-year intervals, proclaimed one for 1423, thus dating it from 1390, and simply not counting the year 1400. Again, there seems to be no bull for this Holy Year, but a tradition was to begin this Holy Year that has continued to this day: Pope Martin opened a Holy Door at the basilica of St. John Lateran.

Nicholas V, considered the first Humanist Pope, did count the Jubilee Year 1400 and, preferring to adhere to the fifty-year intervals, called one for 1450, the first in the early Renaissance period.

It was Pope Nicholas who introduced the custom of a Pontiff greeting the faithful in St. Peter's Square on Sundays and holidays, and it was he who made canonizations and beatifications a regular part of Jubilee celebrations.

Twenty years later, in 1470, Pope Paul II issued a bull declaring that Holy Years would, starting in 1475, be celebrated at twenty-five-year intervals. Except for extraordinary Holy Years, that period is still respected today. Paul II did not live to see the 1475 Jubilee: that was inaugurated by his successor, Pope Sixtus IV (who gave his name to the Sistine Chapel, which he built in 1473). Pope Sixtus also issued orders that Rome be improved and beautified. In fact, one of the city's better-known bridges, Ponte Sisto, is named for this Pontiff. One novelty of this Holy Year was the use of the newly invented printing press to print the Bull of Indiction. It was also used to print information for pilgrims, such as the times and places of Holy Year ceremonies.

The Holy Year 1500 definitively ushered in the custom of opening a Holy Door on Christmas Eve and closing it the following year on Christmas Day. Pope Alexander VI opened the first Holy Door in St. Peter's Basilica, and his legates opened doors on the other three papal basilicas. Alexander created a new opening in the portico of St. Peter's and commissioned a door made of marble for the occasion. It was 3.5 meters high and 2.2 meters wide (11 feet by 7 feet) and lasted until 1618, when another door was installed in the new basilica. That door was replaced in 1950 by a bronze door, which is still in use. Michelangelo's *Pietà* was completed for this Holy Year and placed in a side chapel.

Pope Clement VII opened the Holy Year 1525 in the shadow of the Protestant Reformation. The atmosphere was quite tense, and the Holy Year took place in a very understated way, with far fewer pilgrims than normal coming from abroad.

The following Holy Year, 1550, was marked by the tensions of the Counter-Reformation and the infamous Sack of Rome in 1527. It took place during the Council of Trent (1545-1563), convened by Pope Paul III to help ease those tensions. Paul died in 1549, and his successor, Pope Julius III, immediately proclaimed the Holy Year after his election on February 22, 1550. Two future saints—Ignatius of Loyola and Philip Neri—participated in this Jubilee. That same year, the Pope gave his approval to the order founded by St. Ignatius: the Society of Jesus, or the Jesuits.

Pope Gregory XIII proclaimed the Holy Year 1575 with a bull issued on the feast of the Ascension and read again on the last Sunday of Advent, a practice that continues today. This was indeed a year for jubilation as the Council of Trent had been brought to a successful conclusion twelve years earlier and Rome has been restored and embellished following the sack of the city. Pilgrims flocked to the Eternal City in 1575: some accounts put the number at three hundred thousand. During his pontificate, Pope Gregory reformed the calendar, founded the papal observatory and the Gregorian University, and laid out Via Merulana, which connects the basilicas of St. John Lateran and St. Mary Major. Another street, Via Gregoriana, bears his name.

Pope Clement VIII was Pontiff during the Holy Year 1600, which, chronicles tell us, had the most massive ever participation by pilgrims. The Pope, in fact, instituted two commissions of cardinals to whom he entrusted the ceremonial and logistical aspects of the Jubilee. Clement VIII was the pilgrim par excellence: not only did he assiduously visit Rome's basilicas — history tells us he fulfilled sixty visits — he personally attended to assisting pilgrims and donated large sums of his personal money to this end. During Lent he invited twelve poor people to eat meals with him.

The Holy Year 1625 was celebrated in the new St. Peter's Basilica, although it was only officially dedicated by Pope Urban VIII on November 18, 1626. This is the same date on which the old basilica was supposedly dedicated in 326. This celebration took place during the Thirty Years' War (1618-1648). Due to a flood that had made St. Paul's Basilica unusable, the Pope replaced it with Santa Maria in Trastevere and personally opened the Holy Door. The Pope also issued an order extending the spiritual effects of a Holy Year to all who would be unable to participate but who wished to do so: old people, the ill, cloistered religious, and prisoners. Roman Pontiffs since then have respected this disposition.

Pope Innocent X proclaimed the Holy Year 1650, the first of the High Baroque era, and a period of relative peace. The Pope had the Lateran basilica rebuilt in the new Baroque style, making it lose much of its characteristics of an early Christian basilica.

Jubilees in History

The Jubilee Year 1675, proclaimed by Clement X, is often linked to Queen Christina of Sweden. In 1654 the queen had converted to Catholicism, renounced the throne, and moved to Rome. Considered a symbol of the Faith, she was active in ecclesial events, constantly attending papal and other ceremonies, but became better known for her charitable work, most especially during the Holy Year. Her personal library became celebrated worldwide, and after her death in 1689, it was given to the Vatican Library.

The 1675 Jubilee Year was also noted as being the year in which Theatine Fr. Carlo Tommasi obtained permission from the Pope to dedicate the Coliseum to the memory of martyrs. Among the canonizations that took place in 1675 were those of Gaetano da Thiene, founder of the Theatines; Rose of Lima, the first saint of Latin America; and Francesco Borgia, a superior general of the Jesuits.

As happened in prior Jubilees, the preparatory period for the 1675 Jubilee saw Rome enriched by artistic works. Bernini, in particular, although he was seventy-seven at the time of the Jubilee, had planned St. Peter's Square and the portico of the basilica as well as the Scala Regia of the Apostolic Palaces, the Church of St. Andrew at the Quirinale, the Fabric of St. Peter's and the elephant that still supports the obelisk in the Piazza della Minerva. Especially for the Holy Year he designed the gilded bronze tabernacle for the Blessed Sacrament Chapel in St. Peter's.

The Holy Year of 1700 was the Jubilee of two popes. The much-loved Pope of the Enlightenment, Innocent XII, called the Jubilee in 1699 but was too ill on Christmas Eve to open the Holy Door. This was done by his delegate, Cardinal Emanuele Bouillon. Although Innocent was eighty-six at the time of the Jubilee, he fulfilled many works of piety throughout the year. He died in

A HOLY YEAR IN ROME

September 1700. On November 23, Pope Clement XI was elected, and it was he who—just a month and a day later—would close the Holy Door.

Only a month after his election on May 29, 1724, Pope Benedict XIII, a Dominican who, upon his election, asked permission from his superiors to accept the nomination, proclaimed the Holy Year 1725. A simple, humble, austere man, and a pastor first and foremost, Benedict, as the bishop of Benevento, Italy, had had direct experience in preparing pilgrims for the Jubilee Year 1700. Thus, he was no stranger to the preparations for his first Jubilee as Pope.

It is recorded that Pope Benedict asked that the Holy Year 1725 be celebrated in a very rigorous and spiritual way, characterized by self-denial, penance, prayer, and simple, not ostentatious, liturgical ceremonies. Sacred should prevail over profane—as had not always happened in the past. The Holy Father himself became the model pilgrim and man of prayer and penance.

The Jubilee Year 1725 was marked, as were others, by canonizations and beatifications (including Luigi Gonzaga), and an increase in the artistic patrimony: the renowned Spanish Steps at Trinità dei Monti in the heart of Rome, the work of Francesco de Sanctis, were inaugurated.

On May 5, 1749, Benedict XIV issued the papal bull *Peregrinantes a Domino*, which called for the eighteenth Jubilee Year in Church history. This was the first such bull ever to be addressed not only to Catholics, but to heretics and schismatics as well, inviting everyone to a year of penance. To predispose and prepare pilgrims for the 1750 Jubilee, the Pope also issued a series of encyclicals, explaining the meaning of a Holy Year and how to obtain indulgences. Greatly concerned with the spiritual preparation necessary for a Jubilee, he also laid out precise rules of conduct for the clergy. In his writings he exhorted pastors to "keep churches clean and decent," and to be dignified and diligent at all times.

Before closing the Holy Door on Christmas Day 1750, Pope Benedict published the bull *Benedictus Deus*, in which he extended this Holy Year throughout 1751 for those who had been in some way impeded from coming to Rome in 1750. Almost simultaneously his encyclical *Celebrationem magni* was published, extending Holy Year indulgences to the entire Christian world, on the condition that certain works of charity were performed. Such extensions had been granted in the past, but only after bishops had requested a Pontiff to do so. This time, it had been Benedict's initiative.

The Jubilee Year 1775 marked the second time that one Pope announced a Holy Year and another brought it to completion. Clement XIV, who had proclaimed this Holy Year, died on September 22, 1774. His successor, Pius VI, opened the Holy Door on Christmas Eve and closed it a year later.

Pius VII was prevented from calling a Holy Year in 1800 because of the political climate in Europe and the difficult situation the Church found herself in during the Napoleonic rule.

Pope Leo XII proclaimed the 1825 Jubilee Year. As St. Paul's had been destroyed by fire in 1823, he substituted this church as one of the obligatory destinations for pilgrims with the church of Santa Maria in Trastevere.

No Jubilee was held in 1850 because of the troubled political situation on the Italian peninsula, including the Papal States, and because of the temporary exile of Pope Pius IX. The Papal States had been under the authority of the papacy from 754 to 1870, thus making the Pope a sovereign. In the nineteenth century, a movement for the unification of Italy—and against papal temporal power—had begun, and by 1870 all papal territory was lost. Actually, Pius IX did proclaim a Jubilee Year, but there were no ceremonies to open or close the Holy Door due to the occupation of Rome by King Victor Emmanuel.

Although political circumstances in the now unified kingdom of Italy made it impossible to hold a Holy Year in 1875, Pope Pius IX proclaimed one in an encyclical dated December 24, 1874, extending it to the whole world. No Holy Doors were opened and closed, and no pilgrims came, but this year has come to be celebrated in the annals of Jubilees.

The Holy Year 1900, the twenty-second such celebration, was declared by Pope Leo XIII. In his bull promulgating the Holy Year, Leo XIII, then ninety years old, reminisced about his participation in a Jubilee seventy-five years earlier and about the many negative changes that had taken place since, including the loss of the Papal States and restricting popes to living in the Vatican.

Although this was the first Holy Year celebrated following the integration of the Papal States into Italy, it was endorsed by the Italian government and by King Umberto I, who, however, was assassinated in Monza in July of 1900. It was a Holy Year of new technology and newer, faster ways to travel. Great and enthusiastic crowds came to Rome, and, to help accommodate the growing numbers, St. Martha's Hospice was built in the Vatican and took care of forty thousand pilgrims. The Jubilee was marked by the canonizations of John Baptiste de la Salle and Rita da Cascia, by the first Assembly of the Episcopacy of South America, which took place in the Vatican, and by the building of St. Anselm Church on the Aventine. A particular novelty was linked to the ceremony of closing the Holy Door: twenty bricks from as many Italian mountains, each of which had a statue of the Redeemer built on it during the Holy Year, were walled up in the Holy Door.

Jubilees in History

The Jubilee Year 1925 was proclaimed by Pope Pius XI and, following so shortly upon the heels of World War I, was an especially joyful occasion. It is said that the Pope rejoiced because of the presence of people from so many countries throughout the world, with the notable exception of Russia. And, for the first time, statistics are available on the number of pilgrims: 582,234 came to Rome.

Pius XI also resolved any discussion over the exact number of ordinary Holy Years that had taken place, when he said in December 1925: "The twenty-third Holy Year is drawing to a close." He thus included Holy Year 1875. During this year, Sts. Theresa of the Child Jesus, Peter Canisius, the Cure d'Ars, John Vianney, and John Eudes were canonized. Bernadette of Lourdes was beatified. It was Pope Pius who introduced the now commonplace weekly general audience. He also revived a custom that had been disallowed since 1870: the *Urbi et Orbi* (to the city and to the world) blessing from the central loggia of St. Peter's Basilica.

This twentieth-century Pope was the first of two popes ever to have opened a Holy Door twice: Pius XI did so in 1925 and again in 1933, when he called a Holy Year to celebrate the reconciliation in 1929 between the Italian State and the Vatican (which resulted in the creation of the sovereign Vatican City State on February 11 that same year). Seeking a religious justification to celebrate this Church-state reconciliation, the Pope consulted the rector of the Biblical Institute, who told him that 1933 would mark the 1,900th anniversary of the Redemption and would thus be an appropriate occasion for a Jubilee.

St. John Paul II was the second Pope to open Holy Doors twice: for the 1983 Holy Year marking the 1,950th anniversary of the Redemption and again for the Jubilee Year 2000.

A HOLY YEAR IN ROME

A number of firsts marked this 1933 Holy Year. It was the first extraordinary Jubilee in history and also the first to celebrate the Redemption (nineteen hundred years), and not Christ's birth. Importantly, the ceremony of opening the Holy Door was transmitted by radio, Vatican Radio having been set up two years earlier by the discoverer of radio, Guglielmo Marconi. The Holy Door was opened on Passion Sunday 1933 and closed on Passion Monday a year later. And, for the first time since the end of papal temporal power, a Pope could celebrate Holy Year liturgies outside of St. Peter's Basilica. Pius XI, in fact, led processions to the three other major basilicas in Rome.

Pope Pius XII in May 1949, with the bull *Jubilaeum maximum*, proclaimed the Holy Year 1950, the twenty-fourth Holy Year in history. This would truly be a year of jubilation, following as it did so shortly upon the ravages of World War II. Pius XII was called the Pope of Peace, and it is said that his presence in the See of Peter, as much as the Holy Year itself, attracted nearly three million pilgrims to Rome. The broad and beautiful Via della Conciliazione, leading from the Tiber to St. Peter's Square, was completed for this Jubilee: it was named to mark the reconciliation that took place in 1929 between the Vatican and Italy.

This was also the year that saw the installation of a new Holy Door on St. Peter's Basilica, the door that is still used today. This door was funded by the diocese of Basel, Switzerland, in thanksgiving for having been spared devastation during the war and to honor Pius XII. In between the sixteen panels, described earlier, are the coats of arms of the popes who had opened or closed Holy Doors in previous years.

Vincent Pallotti was beatified this year, and Maria Goretti was canonized, but the culminating point of the 1950 Jubilee was the proclamation in St. Peter's Square on November 1, the feast of All

Saints, of the dogma of Mary's Assumption into Heaven. Just over a month later, the Pope, in his Christmas message, announced the rediscovery of St. Peter's tomb through recent excavations. Today, the tomb of the first Apostle and Pope can be seen when one visits the *scavi*, or excavations, under the Grottoes of St. Peter's Basilica. Tours to the *scavi* are by appointment only and are arranged for small groups by writing to the Ufficio Scavi, Reverenda Fabbrica di San Pietro, Vatican City, 00120 (see my chapter for information on visiting the Vatican and tips for tourists).

The Holy Year 1975 marked the tenth anniversary of the closing of Vatican Council II (1962-1965). Pope Paul VI announced this celebration in his weekly general audience of May 9, 1973, answering those who in recent years had questioned whether a Holy Year was an anachronism.

In his apostolic exhortation *Gaudete in Domino*, the Holy Father asked that this Jubilee Year be a period of joy, conversion, reconciliation, and renewal. Television brought many Holy Year events into homes around the world, and the airplane, by now a common means of transportation, brought millions (between eight and nine million) of faithful to Rome. Elizabeth Ann Seton, the first American-born saint and a convert to Catholicism, was canonized in 1975, as was Irish martyr Oliver Plunkett. Great attention was given this year to ecumenism, to youth, and to women as the Jubilee coincided with the International Woman's Year proclaimed by the United Nations.

Two extraordinary Jubilees have since been celebrated: Pope John Paul II proclaimed 1983-1984 as A Jubilee Year of Redemption, marking 1,950 years since the death of Christ, and extended it to the entire world; and he declared a Marian Year for 1987-1988 and on March 25, 1987, issued an encyclical entitled *On the Blessed Virgin Mary in the Life of the Pilgrim Church.*

A HOLY YEAR IN ROME

The 1983-1984 year began on March 25, the feast of the Annunciation. During that year the first World Youth Day was held in Rome, on Palm Sunday 1984. The Pope also baptized twenty-seven catechumens that year and held numerous beatification and canonization ceremonies, including one in which he proclaimed the friar-painter Fra Angelico Blessed and named him Patron of Artists.

The Marian Year began on Pentecost 1987 and concluded on the feast of the Assumption, August 15, 1988. Pope John Paul II wished this year to be a special prelude to the Great Jubilee of the Year 2000, the twenty-sixth ordinary Jubilee in Church history.

The Great Jubilee Year 2000 saw twenty-eight million pilgrims come to Rome for events that took place almost daily, it seemed, in the Vatican. Many, if not most, weeks saw two general audiences: the traditional midweek audience on Wednesdays and additional audiences on Saturdays. In addition, there were special Jubilee days for children, the Roman Curia, sports people, workers, priests, prisoners, bishops, families, and government leaders and politicians.

Pope John Paul traveled to Mount Sinai, to the Holy Land, and to Fátima. At the end of the May 13 beatification ceremony in Fátima of Francesco and Jacinta Marto, Cardinal Angelo Sodano announced that the "third part" of the secret of Fátima would be made public.

Other events of the Great Jubilee Year 2000: the inauguration of the new entrance of the Vatican Museums; the Day of Pardon, the canonization of Polish Blessed Maria Faustina Kowalska; John Paul II's lunch with 200 poor and homeless people; the beatification of five Venerable Servants of God, including Pope Pius IX and Pope John XXIII; and the canonization of 123 Blesseds, including 120 martyrs in China.

A HISTORICAL PERSPECTIVE

1300	Pope Boniface VIII declares the first Jubilee in history.
1309-1377	Papacy in Avignon, France. Seven popes reigned there due to unsettled conditions in Rome.
1311-1312	Ecumenical Council of Vienna.
1321	Death of Dante Alighieri (b. 1265), a year after finishing the allegorical epic poem *The Divine Comedy*.
1337-1453	Hundred Years' War, a series of wars between France and England.
1347-1350	Black Death sweeps over Europe.
1350	Celebration of second Jubilee (Clement VI).
1374	Death of Petrarch, credited with founding the intellectual and artistic movement called Humanism.
1377	Return of the papacy to Rome. Popes moved to the Vatican in 1378. Start of Western, or Great, Schism, which divided Christendom into diverse loyalties, when two, and eventually three popes fought for control of the Church.

A HOLY YEAR IN ROME

1390	Third regular Jubilee, called by Pope Urban V, who died before the year opened. This fell to his successor Boniface IX.
1400	Boniface IX celebrates the fourth Jubilee, continuing the tradition of celebrating a Holy Year at the start of every century.
1409	Council of Pisa, attempt to end Western Schism.
1414-1418	Council of Pisa resumes; ends Great Schism.
1421	Joan of Arc burned at the stake.
1423	Fifth regular Jubilee, proclaimed by Pope Martin V. First Holy Door opened at St. John Lateran.
1431-1445	Ecumenical Council of Florence. Affirms primacy of Pope over councils.
1450	Sixth Jubilee. Nicholas V declares the first Jubilee of the early Renaissance.
1452	Birth of Leonardo da Vinci (d. 1519).
1456	First printed version of the Bible, following Gutenberg's invention of movable type.
1466	Birth of Erasmus, Dutch theologian, scholar, and writer (d. 1536).

1475   Seventh regular Jubilee. In 1470 Paul II
       had issued a bull declaring that Holy Years,
       starting in 1475, would be celebrated at
       twenty-five-year intervals. The 1475 Jubilee
       was inaugurated by his successor, Sixtus
       IV. Michelangelo is born (d. 1564).

1476   Sixtus IV approves observance throughout
       the Church of the feast of the Immaculate
       Conception on December 8.

1483   Birth of the painter Raphael (d. 1520)
       and Martin Luther (d. 1546).

1492   Christopher Columbus discovers the Americas.
       Renaissance period in full bloom: began in
       fourteenth-century Florence and extended
       throughout Europe by the seventeenth century.

1500   Eighth Jubilee. Pope Alexander VI ushers in
       the Jubilee and opens a Holy Door for the
       first time in St. Peter's Basilica. Pontifical
       legates open Holy Doors at the other three
       papal basilicas (St. Mary Major, St. John
       Lateran and St. Paul Outside-the-Walls).

1506   Pope Julius II establishes Pontifical Swiss Guards.

1512-1517   Ecumenical Council of the Lateran.

1517	Start of the Reformation, when Catholic monk Martin Luther nailed his 95 Theses, calling for reformation in the Church, to the door of the cathedral at Wittenberg. Luther was excommunicated in 1521. Leads to birth of Lutheranism.
1525	Ninth regular Jubilee, declared by Pope Clement VII.
1527	Sack of Rome. One hundred twenty-seven Swiss Guards die defending Clement VII when Rome is invaded.
1533	Henry VIII divorces Catherine of Aragon, remarries, and is excommunicated.
1534	The Society of Jesus (Jesuit Order) is founded by St. Ignatius of Loyola. The order's constitutions are approved in 1540. Henry VIII of England decrees the Act of Supremacy, with which he rejects papal supremacy and declares the sovereign as head of the Church in England. Henry died in 1547.
1545-1564	Ecumenical Council of Trent. Issued numerous decrees on doctrinal matters and instituted many reforms within the Church.
1550	Tenth Jubilee, proclaimed by Pope Julius III.

1558   Start of the reign of Elizabeth I of England and Ireland. The Church of England (Anglican Church), which broke from Rome, takes definitive form. Elizabeth is excommunicated in 1570.

1575   Eleventh regular Jubilee, proclaimed by Gregory XIII.

1582   Gregorian Calendar, named for Gregory XIII, goes into effect. Death of St. Teresa of Ávila, Spanish Carmelite, mystic, and writer.

1591   Death of St. John of the Cross, Carmelite and founder of Discalced Carmelites.

1595   Death of St. Philip Neri, founder of the Congregation of the Oratory (Oratorians).

1598   Birth of Gian Lorenzo Bernini, sculptor, architect, and painter (d. 1680).

1599   Birth of Francesco Borromini, Italian architect and sculptor (d. 1667).

1600   Twelfth Jubilee, called by Clement VIII.

1622   Death of St. Francis de Sales, bishop of Geneva.

1625	Thirteenth Jubilee, proclaimed by Urban VIII. The Vincentians founded by St. Vincent de Paul, who founded the Sisters of Charity in 1633 and died in 1660.
1626	On November 18, Pope Urban VIII officially dedicates the new St. Peter's Basilica.
1642	Death of Galileo Galilei, who was censured by the Holy Office for his belief in a heliocentric (sun-centered) universe. The Church found in his favor and closed the case in 1992.
1643	End of the Thirty Years' War.
1650	Fourteenth regular Jubilee, declared by Innocent X.
1675	Fifteenth Jubilee, proclaimed by Clement X.
1700	Sixteenth regular Jubilee, called by eighty-six-year-old Innocent XII. It was closed by his successor, Clement XI.
1720	St. Paul of the Cross founded the Passionists.
1725	Seventeenth Jubilee, proclaimed by Dominican Pope Benedict XIII.
1732	St. Alphonsus de Liguori founds the Redemptorists.

1750   Eighteenth regular Jubilee,
       declared by Benedict XIV.

1773   Clement XIV issues a brief of
       suppression against the Jesuits. The
       Society of Jesus is restored in 1814.

1775   Nineteenth Jubilee, proclaimed by Clement
       XIV, although his successor, Pius VI, opened
       the Holy Door on Christmas Eve 1774.

1776   Signing of the Declaration of Independence
       of the United States of America.

1789   Start of the French Revolution and
       persecution of the Church in France. First
       Amendment to the U.S. Constitution
       guarantees religious freedom. This century
       is called the Age of Enlightenment.

1800   No Jubilee is held because of the political
       climate in Europe and the difficult situation
       of the Church under Napoleonic rule.
       Napoleon's troops had occupied Rome. Pius
       VII, elected in Venice in 1800, was held
       captive by Napoleon and brought to France,
       where he remained in exile until 1814.
       Napoleon himself died a year later in exile.

1825   Twentieth Jubilee, proclaimed by Pope Leo XII.

1848	Communist Manifesto issued.
1850	No Jubilee held, due to the difficult political situation on the Italian peninsula (including the Papal States) and to the temporary exile of Pope Pius IX. The hierarchy is restored in England, and the first archbishop of Westminster is named.
1854	Pius IX proclaims the dogma of the Immaculate Conception.
1858	Lourdes, France: the Blessed Virgin Mary appears to St. Bernadette Soubirous.
1870-1871	Victor Emmanuel II of Sardinia crowned king of a unified Italy, after marching on Rome in 1870 and confiscating the Papal States a year later.
1875	Twenty-first regular Jubilee. Pius IX proclaims a Holy Year throughout the world. Although political circumstances made it impossible for the Jubilee to be held—no Holy Doors were opened, no ceremonies were held, and few, if any pilgrims came—this Jubilee is nonetheless counted in Church annals.
1878	Death of Pius IX; longest pontificate in history: thirty-one years.

1881	First International Eucharistic Congress is held in Lille, France.
1900	Twenty-second Jubilee, proclaimed by ninety-year-old Pope Leo XIII, noted for his encyclical *Rerum Novarum*.
1903	Death of Leo XIII; second-longest pontificate: twenty-five years.
1911	Founding of the Maryknolls (Catholic Foreign Mission Society of America), the first such U.S.-founded society.
1914-1918	World War I.
1917	Our Lady appears to three children in Fátima, Portugal. Bolsheviks take power in Russia.
1918	*Code of Canon Law* is promulgated in the Western Church.
1925	Twenty-third regular Jubilee, proclaimed by Pius XI.
1929	Vatican City State is created on February 11 with the signing of the Lateran Pacts between the Holy See and Italy, settling the famous Roman Question, which arose with the confiscation of the Papal States in 1871.

1933	Adolf Hitler's rise to power in Germany. Pius XI calls for an extraordinary Holy Year to commemorate the nineteenth centenary of Christ's death.
1936-1939	Civil War in Spain.
1939-1945	World War II.
1940	Start of communist domination in Eastern and Central Europe.
1950	Twenty-fourth regular Jubilee, proclaimed by Pius XII. He also proclaimed the dogma of the Assumption of the Blessed Virgin Mary.
1962-1965	Vatican Council II was held. This was called by Pope John XXIII, who died in June 1963. His successor, Pope Paul VI, closed the council in December 1965.
1975	Twenty-fifth Jubilee, proclaimed by Paul VI.
1978	The year of three popes: Paul VI died on August 6; John Paul I was elected but died on September 28; Pope John Paul II was elected on October 16, and his pontificate officially began on October 22.

1983   Promulgation of the revised *Code of Canon Law* for the Western Church. John Paul II declares an extraordinary Jubilee for 1983-1984—the Jubilee Year of Redemption—to mark the 1,950 years since Christ's death.

1987-1988   Extraordinary Jubilee, called by Pope John Paul II to mark a Marian Year. On March 25, 1987, he issued the encyclical *On the Blessed Virgin Mary in the Life of the Pilgrim Church*.

1989-1991   Fall of the Iron Curtain and the Communist regimes in Central and Eastern Europe.

1991   Promulgation of the Code of Canons for the Oriental Churches.

1992   Promulgation of the new *Catechism of the Catholic Church*.

1994   Pope John Paul II issues the apostolic letter *Tertio Millennio Adveniente* (On the Threshold of the Third Millennium) in November, officially calling for the twenty-sixth regular Jubilee to be held in the year 2000 and outlining the preparatory periods for that Jubilee.

1997   First immediate preparatory year for the Jubilee Year 2000, dedicated to Jesus Christ.

A HOLY YEAR IN ROME

1998	Second preparatory year, dedicated to the Holy Spirit.
1999	Third Jubilee preparatory year, dedicated to God the Father.
2000	Twenty-sixth regular Jubilee celebrations officially started when Pope St. John Paul opened the Holy Door of St. Peter's Basilica on Christmas Eve, 1999. The Holy Doors of St. Mary Major and St. John Lateran Basilicas were opened on Christmas Day, 1999, and that of St. Paul Outside-the-Walls was opened on January 18, 2000, the traditional start of the annual Week of Prayer for Christian Unity; opening services are always held in this basilica.

Chapter IV

A PAPAL SURPRISE — A JUBILEE YEAR OF MERCY

On March 13, 2015, the second anniversary of his election, Pope Francis announced the celebration of an extraordinary Holy Year, calling it a Jubilee of Mercy. At the very start of 2015, the Holy Father had stated: "This is the time of mercy. It is important that the lay faithful live it and bring it into different social environments. Go forth!"

The Jubilee announcement was made as he preached a homily for the penitential liturgy that opened the "24 Hours for the Lord." This is an initiative of the Pontifical Council for Promoting the New Evangelization that advocates the opening of churches throughout the world for an extended period for the purpose of inviting people to the celebration of the sacrament of Reconciliation.

The theme for this year has been taken from the letter of St. Paul to the Ephesians, "God rich in mercy" (see Eph. 2:4).

In his March 13 homily, the Holy Father said:

> This year again, on the eve of the Fourth Sunday of Lent, we are gathered to celebrate the penitential liturgy. We

are united with the many Christians who, today, in every part of the world, have accepted the invitation to live this moment as a sign of the Lord's goodness. The Sacrament of Reconciliation, indeed, allows us to draw near to the Father with trust to have the certainty of his forgiveness. He is truly "rich in mercy" and extends it abundantly upon those who appeal to Him with a sincere heart.

And he ended his homily with the surprise announcement, truly a very well-kept secret:

> Dear brothers and sisters, I have often thought of how the Church may render more clear her mission to be a witness to mercy; and we have to make this journey. It is a journey that begins with spiritual conversion. Therefore, I have decided to announce an *Extraordinary Jubilee* that will have at its center the mercy of God. It will be a *Holy Year of Mercy*. We want to live in the light of the word of the Lord: "Be merciful, even as your Father is merciful" (cf. Lk 6:36). And this especially applies to confessors! So much mercy!
>
> This Holy Year will commence on December 8, 2015, the Solemnity of the Immaculate Conception, and will conclude on Sunday, November 20, 2016, the Solemnity of Our Lord Jesus Christ, King of the Universe and living face of the Father's mercy. I entrust the organization of this Jubilee to the Pontifical Council for Promoting the New Evangelization, in order that it may come to life as a new step on the Church's journey in her mission to bring the Gospel of mercy to each person.
>
> I am confident that the whole Church, which is in such need of mercy, for we are sinners, will be able to find in this Jubilee the joy of rediscovering and rendering fruitful

God's mercy, with which we are all called to give comfort to every man and every woman of our time. Do not forget that God *forgives all*, and God *forgives always*. Let us never tire of asking forgiveness. Let us henceforth entrust this Year to the Mother of Mercy, that she turn her gaze upon us and watch over our journey: our penitential journey, our year-long journey with an open heart, to receive the indulgence of God, to receive the mercy of God.

Mercy, of course, has been a hallmark of Francis's papacy. In fact, in what has been called his signature document, the 2013 apostolic exhortation *Evangelii Gaudium*, the term *mercy* appears thirty-two times. We also know mercy is a theme very dear to him, as expressed in the episcopal motto he chose and kept as Pope: *Miserando atque eligendo*, "by having mercy, by choosing him."

In fact, on March 17, 2013, at the first Angelus after his election, the Holy Father stated: "Feeling mercy, this word changes everything. This is the best thing we can feel: it changes the world. A little mercy makes the world less cold and more just. We need to understand properly this mercy of God, this merciful Father who is so patient."

The December 8 opening of the Jubilee will take place on the fiftieth anniversary of the closing of Vatican Council II in 1965. This is of great significance, for it motivates the Church to continue the work begun at Vatican II.

During the Jubilee, the Sunday readings for Ordinary Time will be taken from the Gospel of Luke, the one referred to as "the evangelist of mercy." Dante Alighieri describes him as "*scriba mansuetudinis Christi*," "narrator of the meekness of Christ." There are many well-known parables of mercy presented in the Gospel of Luke: the lost sheep, the lost coin, the merciful father.

A HOLY YEAR IN ROME

The official and solemn announcement of the Holy Year took place with the public proclamation of the Bolla, or Bull of Indiction, in front of the Holy Door on the vigil of Divine Mercy Sunday, April 11, 2015, the feast instituted by St. John Paul II and celebrated on the Sunday after Easter. The twenty-eight-page bull, *Misericordiae Vultus* (*The Face of Mercy*) opens with the declaration, "Jesus is the face of the Father's mercy. These words might well sum up the mystery of the Christian faith."

That presentation took place in the atrium of St. Peter's Basilica when Pope Francis told the faithful that there will be a Jubilee "because this is the time for mercy. It is the favorable time to heal wounds, a time not to be weary of meeting all those who are waiting to see and to touch with their hands the signs of the closeness of God, a time to offer everyone the way of forgiveness and reconciliation."

To one side of the Holy Door, the regent of the Papal Household, Msgr. Leonardo Sapienza, as apostolic protonotary, read various extracts from the official document convoking the extraordinary Holy Year.

The Bull of Indiction was then handed to the four cardinal archpriests of the papal basilicas of Rome: Cardinal Angelo Comastri, archpriest of the Basilica of St. Peter in the Vatican; Cardinal Agostino Vallini, archpriest of the Basilica of St. John Lateran; Cardinal James Michael Harvey, archpriest of St. Paul Outside-the-Walls; and Cardinal Santos Abril y Castello, archpriest of the Basilica of St. Mary Major.

In addition, to expressing his wish that the Extraordinary Jubilee of Mercy be celebrated in Rome and throughout the world, Pope Francis gave a copy of the bull—thus presenting it symbolically to all bishops—to Cardinal Marc Ouellet P.S.S., prefect of the Congregation for Bishops; to Cardinal Fernando Filoni, prefect of the Congregation for the Evangelization of Peoples; and to Cardinal Leonardo Sandri, prefect of the Congregation for the Oriental Churches.

What is a Bull of Indiction?

The term *bull* (from the Latin *bulla*, "bubble," or, more generally, a rounded object) originally indicated the metal capsule used to protect the wax seal attached with a cord to a document of particular importance, to attest to its authenticity and, as a consequence, its authority. Over time, the term began to be used first to indicate the seal, then the document itself, so that nowadays it is used for all documents of special importance that bear, or at least traditionally would have borne, the Pontiff's seal.

The Bull of Indiction (formal announcement or proclamation) of a Jubilee, for instance, in the case of an extraordinary Holy Year, aside from indicating its time, with the opening and closing dates and the main ways in which it will be implemented, constitutes the fundamental document for recognizing the spirit in which it is announced and the intentions and the outcomes hoped for by the Pontiff, who invokes it for the Church.

In the ancient Hebrew tradition, the Jubilee Year, which was celebrated every fifty years, was meant to restore equality among all of the children of Israel, offering new possibilities to families that had lost their property and even their personal freedom. In addition, the Jubilee Year was a reminder to the rich that a time would come when their Israelite slaves would once again become their equals and would be able to reclaim their rights. "Justice, according to the Law of Israel, consisted above all in the protection of the weak" (St. John Paul II, *Tertio Millennio Adveniente* 13).

The Catholic tradition of the Holy Year began with Pope Boniface VIII in 1300. The Pope had envisioned a Jubilee every century. From 1475 onward—in order to allow each generation to experience at least one Holy Year—the ordinary Jubilee was to be celebrated every twenty-five years. However, an Extraordinary Jubilee may be announced on the occasion of an event of particular importance.

The last ordinary Holy Year was the Jubilee of 2000. The custom of calling Extraordinary Jubilees dates back to the sixteenth century. The extraordinary Holy Years that were celebrated during the previous century were those in 1933, proclaimed by Pius XI to celebrate 1,900 years of Redemption, and in 1983, proclaimed by John Paul II on the occasion of the 1,950 years of Redemption. (See my chapter on the History of Jubilees.)

The initial rite of the Jubilee is the opening of the Holy Door. This door is one that is opened only during a Holy Year and remains closed during all other years. This rite of the opening of the Holy Door illustrates symbolically the idea that, during the Jubilee, the faithful are offered an "extraordinary pathway" to salvation.

The first Holy Door to be opened is that of St. Peter's Basilica on December 8, followed by the Holy Door of St. John Lateran and the cathedrals of the world on Sunday, December 13, the Third Sunday of Advent. On Friday, January 1, 2016, the Solemnity of Mary, the Holy Mother of God and the World Day of Peace, the Holy Door will be opened at the Basilica of St. Mary Major. On Monday, January 25, 2016, the feast of the Conversion of St. Paul, the Holy Door of the Basilica of St. Paul Outside-the-Walls, the last of the four papal basilicas, will be opened.

While there are four papal basilicas to be visited on a pilgrimage, there are three additional churches that are considered part of a pilgrim's itinerary: St. Sebastian, Holy Cross in Jerusalem, and St. Lawrence Outside-the-Walls. I describe each of these seven basilicas in a later chapter.

A Papal Surprise

Pope Francis entrusted the Pontifical Council for Promoting the New Evangelization with the organization of the Jubilee of Mercy. The Jubilee website (www.im.va) is in seven languages and includes updates to the Jubilee calendar.

In the Bull of Indiction of the Extraordinary Jubilee of Mercy, *Misericordiae Vultus*, Pope Francis has described the most salient features of mercy, focusing primarily on the theme of the light of Christ's face. Mercy is not an abstract word, but rather a face to recognize, contemplate, and serve. The bull is developed in a Trinitary fashion (nos. 6-9) and extends to a description of the Church as a credible sign of mercy: "Mercy is the very foundation of the Church's life" (no. 10).

Pope Francis indicates the significant phases of the Jubilee. The opening coincides with the fiftieth anniversary of the closing of the Second Vatican Ecumenical Council: "The Church feels a great need to keep this event alive. With the Council, the Church entered a new phase of her history. The Council Fathers strongly perceived, as a true breath of the Holy Spirit, a need to talk about God to men and women of their time in a more accessible way. The walls which too long had made the Church a kind of fortress were torn down and the time had come to proclaim the Gospel in a new way" (no. 4). The conclusion will take place "with the liturgical Solemnity of Christ the King on 20 November 2016. On that day, as we seal the Holy Door, we shall be filled, above all, with a sense of gratitude and thanksgiving to the Most Holy Trinity for having granted us an extraordinary time of grace. We will entrust the life of the Church, all humanity, and the entire cosmos to the Lordship of Christ, asking him to pour out his mercy upon us like the morning dew, so that everyone may work together to build a brighter future" (no. 5).

A special feature of this Holy Year is the fact that it will be celebrated not only in Rome, but also in all the other diocese the world. The Holy Door will be opened by the Pope at St. Peter's on December 8 and, on the following Sunday, in all the churches of the world. Another novelty is that the Pope will grant the possibility of opening the Holy Door also in sanctuaries, where many pilgrims will go in order to pray.

Pope Francis resumes the teaching of St. John XXIII who spoke of the "medicine of Mercy," and of Paul VI, who identified the spirituality of Vatican II with that of the Samaritan. The bull explains, furthermore, various aspects of the Jubilee: firstly, the motto, Merciful Like the Father, then the meaning of pilgrimage and above all the need for forgiveness. The theme that is particularly close to the Pope's heart is found in paragraph 15: the Corporal and Spiritual Works of Mercy are to be resumed in order to "reawaken our conscience, too often grown dull in the face of poverty. And let us enter more deeply into the heart of the Gospel where the poor have a special experience of God's mercy." A further indication is offered by Lent, with the sending out of the "Missionaries of Mercy" (no. 18), a new and original initiative by which the Pope intends to emphasize his pastoral care in a more concrete way. In paragraphs 20 and 21, the Pope considers the theme of the relationship between justice and mercy, showing that he does not stop at a legalistic view, but rather aims at a path that leads to merciful love.

Paragraph 19 is a powerful appeal against organized violence and against those who are "advocates and accomplices" of corruption. The Pope uses strong words to denounce this "festering wound" and insists that during this Holy Year there must be true conversion:

This is the opportune moment to change our lives! This is the time to allow our hearts to be touched! When confronted with evil deeds, even in the face of serious crimes, it is the time to listen to the cry of innocent people who are deprived of their property, their dignity, their feelings, and even their very lives. To stick to the way of evil will only leave one deluded and sad. True life is something entirely different. God never tires of reaching out to us. He is always ready to listen, as I am too, along with my brother bishops and priests. All one needs to do is to accept the invitation to conversion and submit oneself to justice during this special time of mercy offered by the Church. (no. 19)

The granting of indulgences as a traditional theme of the Jubilee year is expressed in paragraph 22. A final original aspect is offered by Pope Francis with regard to mercy as a theme shared also by Jews and Muslims:

I trust that this Jubilee year celebrating the mercy of God will foster an encounter with these religions and with other noble religious traditions; may it open us to even more fervent dialogue so that we might know and understand one another better; may it eliminate every form of closed-mindedness and disrespect, and drive out every form of violence and discrimination. (no. 23)

The Pope's wish is that this year, experienced also in the sharing of divine mercy, may be dedicated to living out in our daily lives the mercy which the Father constantly extends to all of us. In this Jubilee Year, let us allow God to surprise us. He never tires of throwing open the doors of his heart and repeats that he loves us and wants to share his love with us.... In this Jubilee Year, r the Church echo the word of God that resounds strong and as a message and a sign of pardon, strength, aid, and l she never tire of extending mercy, and be ever patien' compassion and comfort. May the Church become the voice of every man and woman, and repeat confidently without end: "Be mindful of your mercy, O Lord, and your steadfast love, for they have been from of old."

The entire document can be found on the Vatican website: http://w2.vatican.va/content/francesco/en/apost_letters/docu-ments/papa-francesco_bolla_20150411_misericordiae-vultus.html.

LETTER OF POPE FRANCIS GRANTING INDULGENCE TO THE FAITHFUL ON THE OCCASION OF THE EXTRA-ORDINARY JUBILEE OF MERCY

To My Venerable Brother Archbishop Rino Fisichella, President of the Pontifical Council for the Promotion of the New Evangelization:

With the approach of the *Extraordinary Jubilee of Mercy* I would like to focus on several points which I believe require attention to enable the celebration of the Holy Year to be for all believers a true moment of encounter with the mercy of God. It is indeed my wish that the Jubilee be a living experience of the closeness of the Father, whose tenderness is almost tangible, so that the faith of every believer may be strengthened and thus testimony to it be ever more effective.

My thought first of all goes to all the faithful who, whether in individual Dioceses or as pilgrims to Rome, will experience the ⁀e of the Jubilee. I wish that the Jubilee Indulgence may reach ⁀ne as a genuine experience of God's mercy, which comes ⁀ch person in the Face of the Father who welcomes and forgives, forgetting completely the sin committed. To experience and obtain the Indulgence, the faithful are called to make a brief pilgrimage to the Holy Door, open in every Cathedral or in the churches designated by the Diocesan Bishop, and in the four Papal Basilicas in Rome, as a sign of the deep desire for true conversion. Likewise, I dispose that the Indulgence may be obtained in the Shrines in which the Door of Mercy is open and in the churches which traditionally are identified as Jubilee Churches. It is important that this moment be linked, first and foremost, to the Sacrament of Reconciliation and to the celebration of the Holy Eucharist with a reflection on mercy. It will be necessary to accompany these celebrations with the profession of faith and with prayer for me and for the intentions that I bear in my heart for the good of the Church and of the entire world.

Additionally, I am thinking of those for whom, for various reasons, it will be impossible to enter the Holy Door, particularly the sick and people who are elderly and alone, often confined to the home. For them it will be of great help to live their sickness and suffering as an experience of closeness to the Lord who in the mystery of his Passion, death and Resurrection indicates the royal road which gives meaning to pain and loneliness. Living with faith and joyful hope this moment of trial, receiving communion or attending Holy Mass and community prayer, even through the various means of communication, will be for them the means of obtaining the Jubilee Indulgence. My thoughts also turn to those incarcerated, whose freedom is limited. The Jubilee Year has always constituted an opportunity for great amnesty, which is intended to include the many people who, despite deserving punishment, have become conscious of the injustice they worked and sincerely w° to re-enter society and make their honest contribution to i⁺ they all be touched in a tangible way by the mercy of th who wants to be close to those who have the greatest need of his forgiveness. They may obtain the Indulgence in the chapels of the prisons. May the gesture of directing their thought and prayer to the Father each time they cross the threshold of their cell signify for them their passage through the Holy Door, because the mercy of God is able to transform hearts, and is also able to transform bars into an experience of freedom.

I have asked the Church in this Jubilee Year to rediscover the richness encompassed by the spiritual and corporal works of mercy. The experience of mercy, indeed, becomes visible in the witness of concrete signs as Jesus himself taught us. Each time that one of the faithful personally performs one or more of these actions, he or she shall surely obtain the Jubilee Indulgence. Hence the commitment to live by mercy so as to obtain the grace of complete and exhaustive forgiveness by the power of the love of the Father who excludes no one. The Jubilee Indulgence is thus full, the fruit of the very event which is to be celebrated and experienced with faith, hope and charity.

Furthermore, the Jubilee Indulgence can also be obtained for the deceased. We are bound to them by the witness of faith and charity that they have left us. Thus, as we remember them in the Eucharistic celebration, thus we can, in the great mystery of the Communion of Saints, pray for them, that the merciful Face of the Father free them of every remnant of fault and strongly embrace them in the unending beatitude.

One of the serious problems of our time is clearly the changed relationship with respect to life. A widespread and insensitive mentality has led to the loss of the proper personal and social sitivity to welcome new life. The tragedy of abortion is experi- by some with a superficial awareness, as if not realizing the harm that such an act entails. Many others, on the other hand, although experiencing this moment as a defeat, believe that they have no other option. I think in particular of all the women who have resorted to abortion. I am well aware of the pressure that has led them to this decision. I know that it is an existential and moral ordeal. I have met so many women who bear in their heart the scar of this agonizing and painful decision. What has happened is profoundly unjust; yet only understanding the truth of it can enable one not to lose hope. The forgiveness of God cannot be denied to one who has repented, especially when that person approaches the Sacrament of Confession with a sincere heart in order to obtain reconciliation with the Father. For this reason too, I have decided, notwithstanding anything to the contrary, to concede to all priests for the Jubilee Year the discretion to absolve of the sin of abortion those who have procured it and who, with contrite heart, seek forgiveness for it. May priests fulfil this great task by expressing words of genuine welcome combined with a reflection that explains the gravity of the sin committed, besides indicating a path of authentic conversion by which to obtain the true and generous forgiveness of the Father who renews all with his presence.

A final consideration concerns those faithful who for various reasons choose to attend churches officiated by priests of the Fraternity of St Pius X. This Jubilee Year of Mercy excludes no one. From various quarters, several Brother Bishops have told me of their good faith and sacramental practice, combined however with an uneasy situation from the pastoral standpoint. I trust that in the near future solutions may be found to recover full communion with the priests and superiors of the Fraternity. In the meantime motivated by the need to respond to the good of these fai through my own disposition, I establish that those who du Holy Year of Mercy approach these priests of the Frat

Pius X to celebrate the Sacrament of Reconciliation shall validly and licitly receive the absolution of their sins.

Trusting in the intercession of the Mother of Mercy, I en-trust the preparations for this Extraordinary Jubilee Year to her protection.

From the Vatican, 1 September 2015
FRANCIS

POPE FRANCIS'S PRAYER
FOR THE JUBILEE

Lord Jesus Christ,
You have taught us to be merciful like the heavenly Father,
and have told us that whoever sees You sees Him.
Show us Your face and we will be saved.
Your loving gaze freed Zacchaeus and Matthew from being
*   enslaved by money;*
the adulteress and Magdalene from seeking happiness only
*   in created things;*
made Peter weep after his betrayal,
and assured Paradise to the repentant thief.
Let us hear, as if addressed to each one of us, the words
*   that You spoke to the Samaritan woman:*
"If you knew the gift of God!"
You are the visible face of the invisible Father,
of the God Who manifests His power above all by
*   forgiveness and mercy:*
let the Church be Your visible face in the world, its Lord
*   risen and glorified.*

A Papal Surprise

You willed that Your ministers would also be clothed in
*   weakness*
in order that they may feel compassion for those in ignorance
*   and error:*
let everyone who approaches them feel sought after, loved,
*   and forgiven by God.*
Send Your Spirit and consecrate every one of us with its
*   anointing,*
so that the Jubilee of Mercy may be a year of grace from
*   the Lord,*
and Your Church, with renewed enthusiasm, may bring
*   good news to the poor,*
proclaim liberty to captives and the oppressed,
and restore sight to the blind.
We ask this through the intercession of Mary, Mother
*   of Mercy,*
You who live and reign with the Father and the Holy Spirit
*   for ever and ever.*
Amen.[1]

Chapter V

THE SEVEN PILGRIMAGE BASILICAS OF ROME

BASILICA OF ST. PETER

Many years ago I heard someone say that architecture is frozen music. If that is so, then St. Peter's Basilica is a symphony. No church, no monument we have ever seen prepares us for the grandeur, glory, and sheer immensity of St. Peter's. More than any church I know, one has to prepare mentally for St. Peter's Basilica.

So, as a fitting prelude, we start our visit with St. Peter's Square, awesome because of its massive size (it can hold several hundred thousand people) as well as its simple beauty. In the center is the Egyptian obelisk brought there in 1588 by Domenico Fontana from its earlier site in Caligula's Circus (inside what is now Vatican City: this site is marked by a granite disk in the pavement near the Canonical Palace, just inside the Arch of the Bells entrance to the Vatican, to the left of the basilica). On either side are two fountains: the one on the right is based on a project by Ca

A HOLY YEAR IN ROME

Maderno in 1613, and the one on the left was added in 1675 by Gian Lorenzo Bernini.

Although the cornerstone for the new St. Peter's Basilica was laid in 1506, completion of the church, the square, and the colonnades lasted well into the next century. The two semicircular colonnades, in fact, with their 284 columns embracing the Baroque-style square, were designed by Bernini between 1656 and 1666, during the papacy of Alexander VII. On the balustrade of the two colonnades are 140 statues of saints, each 3.2 meters high, also designed by Bernini.

Two porphyry disks placed in the pavement between the fountains and the obelisk allow the visitor, when standing on them and glancing from left to right in a panoramic fashion, to view the columns, which are four deep, as if they were a single column—an astonishing feat, indeed a marvel of engineering at the very least.

Five porticoes on the façade of St. Peter's, designed by Carlo Maderno and completed in 1614, welcome us on ground level to the atrium, where five more doors are located. Above the porticoes and atrium is the Hall of Blessings, used for numerous ceremonies. Three balconies or loggias overlook the square from this hall: the central one is used twice a year (on Christmas and Easter) by the Pontiff when he imparts his Urbi et Orbi (to the city and the world) blessing. It is also used when a newly elected Pope appears to greet and bless the faithful for the first time following his election as Bishop of Rome. Atop the façade are thirteen statues, each 5.7 meters high: Christ is at the center, and John the Baptist and eleven Apostles (excluding Peter) are at His sides.

In the nineteenth century, statues of Sts. Peter and Paul were placed at the base of the façade, on either side of Bernini's steps. St. Peter is on the left and St. Paul on the right. St. Peter is holding the keys to the Kingdom, and St. Paul has a sword in his right

70

hand and, in his left, a book with the inscription in Hebrew, "can do all things in him who strengthens me" (Phil. 4:13).

The present basilica was built on the site of the first one. In 324 Constantine, the first Christian emperor, ordered a church built over what was believed to be (and proven so in later years) the burial site of St. Peter. The basilica, with a nave, four aisles, and a courtyard, was completed in 349, about a dozen years after Constantine's death. For almost twelve centuries it withstood the ravages of time, sacking by barbarians, and neglect, until Pope Julius II, who considered the church no longer safe, ordered a new basilica to be constructed. The cornerstone was laid on April 18, 1506.

On November 18, 1626, exactly 1,300 years to the day that the first basilica was dedicated, and 120 years after work had begun on the new basilica, Pope Urban VIII dedicated St. Peter's. In that century-plus interval, some of the greatest artists, architects and sculptors known to mankind contributed to the design and building of the new, majestic St. Peter's: Bernini, Bramante, Michelangelo, Raphael, Sangallo, Giacomo della Porta, Fontana, and Maderno, to name but a few.

We start our visit to this wondrous church in the atrium, which measures 71 meters in length, 13.5 in width and 20 in height and was designed by Maderno. In the center of the floor is an inscription that commemorates the inauguration of Vatican II on October 11, 1962, and the coat of arms of Pope John XXIII, who convened and opened that council.

Five bronze doors lead into the church, only two of which are open to visitors. The central fifteenth-century door from the old St. Peter's, and the one to our extreme left, designed by Giacomo Manzu in 1964 and known as the Door of Death, remain closed. The door to the extreme right, the Holy Door, is opened only during Holy Years.

The four main panels of the central door portray Christ, Mary, and the martyrdoms of Sts. Peter and Paul. Minor panels depict stories from the papacy of Eugene IV (1431-1447), who commissioned the door. Above the door is a restored mosaic, originally made by Giotto for the first Jubilee in 1300. Entitled the *Navicella*, or "little boat," it depicts the boat of the Apostles, and Jesus and St. Peter on the lake of Tiberias.

The ten panels on the Door of Death offer representations of the theme of death. On the reverse side, inside the basilica, John XXIII is depicted receiving the bishops on the first day of the Second Vatican Council.

The door immediately to the left of the central one is called the Door of Good and Evil and is used by visitors to exit St. Peter's. Donated to Pope Paul VI (1963-1978), the panels reflect the struggle between good and evil.

The door between the central one and the Holy Door, used to enter the basilica, was completed in 1965 and is called the Door of the Sacraments. The first panel, on the upper left, portrays an angel announcing the grace of the sacraments. The remaining panels depict the seven sacraments of the Church.

To our extreme right is the Holy Door. This was donated by Swiss Catholics to Pope Pius XII (1939-1958) for the 1950 Holy Year. It was sculpted by Siena artist Vico Consorti and replaced the wood panels of the inner door that had been inaugurated on Christmas Eve 1749 by Benedict XIV. It has sixteen panels, fifteen of which depict scenes from the Old and New Testaments: the expulsion from the Garden of Eden, the Annunciation, the Baptism of Christ, the Good Shepherd, the Prodigal Son, the resurrection of Lazarus, the healing of the paralytic, the adulteress, Peter's denial of the Lord, the repentant thief, the good thief, the doubting Thomas, the sacrament of Penance, the conversion of

St. Paul, and the Resurrection. The last panel is the ope
the Holy Door by Pius XII.

Now, with bated breath, we enter the basilica, which is in t
form of a Latin cross. The first impression is one of utter, total
immensity. Yet, as we slowly walk down the center aisle or nave,
studying the six enormous capitals on our right and left, the eight
intervening arches, the height of the ceiling, the distance to the
stupendous main altar and its stunning baldachin or canopy, designed by Bernini, the number and size of statues, the papal tombs
and side altars, that impression changes to one of magnificent
harmony. Everything is so grand, so well-proportioned, that, in a
sense, the vastness no longer overcomes; rather, it is welcoming
and peaceful.

To describe St. Peter's Basilica in anything less than a small
book is like listening to a handful of musical notes and being told
you have just heard an entire opera. But we'll do our best.

To gain some slight idea of the size of St. Peter's (192.76 meters
long and 58 meters wide, with a 44.50-meter-high vault), look at
the bronze plaques in the very center of the basilica's splendid
marble floor. As we proceed toward the main altar, there are just
over thirty plaques, and each records, in a Latin inscription, the
name and length of other churches in the world, Catholic and
non-Catholic, relative to St. Peter's. The second largest church, for
example, is St. Paul's in London (158.1 meters); the fourth largest
is the Shrine of the Immaculate Conception in Washington, D.C.
(139.14 meters); and the twelfth largest is St. Paul Outside-the-
Walls (127.36 meter) in Rome. Others include the cathedrals of
Reims, Florence, Brussels, Cologne, and Seville, to name a few.

As we stand in the nave, there is a feeling of helplessness, of
"where do I start"? We are taken aback by the magnitude of what
we see, by the gigantic capitals and arches on our right and left, by

.y of the marble floor, by statues, bas-reliefs and stunning ..ics, by the light streaming in through the upper-story win- .ws, by the gloriously canopied main altar and the unparalleled beauty of Michelangelo's dome, supported by four colossal piers, each the height of a three-story building.

First, let us walk slowly up and down the two side aisles, whose beautiful chapels, sculptures, monuments, and mosaics gradually prepare us for the awesome beauty of two of Bernini's master-pieces—the stupendous Altar of the Cathedra, or Chair of Peter, which dominates the apse, and the majestic papal altar in the center of the transept—and for the "heart" of the basilica, the *Confessio*, in front of and beneath the papal altar. The papal altar is so called because only the Pope or someone he delegates may celebrate Mass there.

As we stroll the side aisles, our attention is drawn to the numerous commemorative monuments to the popes, many of whom were instrumental in building and embellishing the basilica. Some of these are the tombs of the 147 popes and other famous people buried in St. Peter's. Others are in the Grotto area beneath the basilica. However, the second altar in each of the side aisles contains the remains of two popes: on our left, St. Pius X (1903-1914) and on our right, St. John Paul II. Pope Innocent XI (1676-1689), the former resident of St. Sebastian's Chapel, was moved closer to the front of the basilica to make room for John Paul II after his beatification in 2011.

Walking along, we also note the thirty-nine niches carved into the columns in the nave, the transept and the apse: these contain statues (most of which date from the eighteenth and nineteenth centuries) of the saints who founded religious orders.

Starting with the left aisle, the first chapel we see is the Baptistry Chapel. It does not have an altar but does contain a red porphyry basin from an ancient Roman tomb and is used to minister the sacrament of Baptism. The mosaic decorations a refer to this sacrament.

The next is the Chapel of the Presentation, under whose main altar is buried Pius X. On our left is a monument to Benedict XV and on our right is one dedicated to John XXIII.

Just after this chapel, at the second column, is the Renaissance monument to Innocent VIII (1484-1492), the only one from the former basilica that is preserved in St. Peter's. The Pope is shown holding the spearhead that wounded Christ, a relic donated to the Pontiff by Sultan Bayazid II and preserved in one of the four piers supporting the dome and framing the main altar.

The Chapel of the Choir, enclosed by a Baroque bronze gate, is next. It takes its name from the fact that major Catholic churches are administered by canons who, on certain days and at certain hours, recite together the Liturgy of the Hours. This is the last chapel in that part of the basilica designed by Maderno between 1606 and 1614.

The left aisle ends with the large mosaic reproduction of Raphael's painting of the Transfiguration, now housed in the Vatican Museums. All the mosaics in St. Peter's have been entrusted—original designs or repairs—to the Vatican Mosaic Studio, founded at the end of the sixteenth century, but only officially instituted by Pope Benedict XIII in 1727. The Mosaic Studio is administered by the Reverenda Fabbrica di San Pietro (the Fabric of St. Peter's), which cares for the maintenance of the basilica.

The word *Fabbrica* was originally used to denote the main workshop area for the building of a new church, where designs were made, models were created, and materials used in building were kept. The Fabric of St. Peter's, created by Paul VI in 1967, actually traces its roots to Pope Julius II, who, as we saw earlier, ordered the

...ding of the new St. Peter's in 1506 and granted special favors ... all those who contributed to its building. Pope Clement VII formalized this when he created a college of administrators whose duty it was to help build and administer the basilica.

Crossing over to the right aisle (we will return to the transept and apse), and walking toward the basilica entrance, we come back to that part of the basilica built by Carlo Maderno.

Halfway up the aisle is the Chapel of the Blessed Sacrament, enclosed by a bronze Baroque gate and heavy red drapes. This chapel is strictly for those who wish to pray, and no tour groups are brought into it. The tabernacle on the main altar was designed by Bernini and has the shape of a round temple. Behind this is the only remaining painting in St. Peter's—Pietro da Corona's 1669 depiction of the Trinity.

On the column opposite this chapel is a monument to Matilda of Canossa, an eleventh-century papal benefactress whose remains are in the sarcophagus we see. On this is depicted Emperor Henry IV of Germany at the castle of Canossa on January 28, 1077, kneeling at the feet of Pope Gregory VII, who had excommunicated him.

The next chapel we see is dedicated to St. Sebastian, whose mosaic altarpiece represents the saint's death. This is a copy of the original, executed by Domenichino in 1613 and transferred in 1730 to the Church of Santa Maria degli Angeli (St. Mary of the Angels, located in the center of Rome, in what used to be the baths of Diocletian). St. John Paul II is buried here.

Exiting this chapel, we see a pillar on our right with a monument to Queen Christina of Sweden, who, after renouncing the throne and her Lutheran faith, converted to Catholicism, eventually residing in Rome. She died at the age of sixty-three in 1689 and is buried in the Vatican Grottoes.

The last chapel on our right is, without doubt, the most vr
for it houses the basilica's most famous work of art, Michelanger
Pietà. Commissioned by the French ambassador to Rome in 1498,
when Michelangelo was only twenty-three, the 1.74-meter-high
statue was sculpted from a single piece of marble and is believed
to be the only work the artist signed. The story goes that, when
the completed sculpture was placed in the chapel of the French
Kings in the left arm of the transept before the construction of
the new basilica, Michelangelo overheard two prelates discussing it
and wondering who had sculpted it. To leave no doubt in anyone's
mind, Michelangelo entered the basilica that night and carved his
name on the sash that crosses over Mary's left shoulder. The dome
of this chapel (one of ten "mini" domes in the basilica) has the
only remaining ceiling fresco in St. Peter's.

Our attention now turns to what is assuredly the most overwhelming part of St. Peter's: the apse and transept. Approaching
from the left aisle, we skirt for a moment the triple wonders of the
Altar of the Chair, the Papal Altar and baldachin, and the dome.

On our left is the richly decorated Clementine Chapel, named
for Pope Clement VIII who had it embellished for the Jubilee of
1600, below whose altar is preserved the body of Pope Gregory
the Great.

A short distance on is the entrance to the Sacristy and Treasury of St. Peter's. The main sacristy is an octagonal-shaped room,
inaugurated in 1784, whose fluted columns were brought from
Hadrian's Villa in Tivoli, not far from Rome. Adjacent to this, on
the east side, is the Sacristy of the Canons. On the west side are
the ten rooms of the Treasury, a historical-artistic museum containing a collection of monuments (such as the bronze tomb of
Sixtus IV), liturgical vestments and vessels, and other holy objects,
including pectoral crosses, reliquaries, and a copy of the Chair of

, said to have been used by the first Pope but what is actu-
y the oakwood throne donated to Pope John VIII (872-882) by
Emperor Charles the Bald, on the occasion of his coronation in
St. Peter's on Christmas Day 875.

We now move to the apse and to another Bernini masterpiece,
the splendid Altar of the Cathedra, or Altar of the Chair, executed
between 1658 and 1666. A bronze throne above the marble altar
that encases the Chair of Peter dominates the apse. It is supported
by four statues of bishops: two Fathers of the Latin Church, Sts.
Ambrose and Augustine, and two from the Greek Church, Sts.
Athanasius and John Chrysostom. Above them, in the midst of
gilded clouds, flights of angels, and rays of sun is the Holy Spirit,
illuminated by an alabaster window. Notwithstanding its appearance of lightness and harmony, records show that more than 120
tons of bronze were used for this breathtaking monument. There
are frequent Masses and vespers at this altar. The feast of the Chair
of Peter is February 22.

We return to the pièce de résistance, the papal altar of the
Confessio, or confession, so called because it was erected over the
burial place of one who confessed his faith to the point of martyrdom. The altar drew our attention from the first moment we
entered the basilica, but now we are truly enraptured as we stand
in front of it, studying its grandiose, yet simple majesty, reflecting
on the many papal Masses that have been celebrated there, and
pondering the man buried below, the simple fisherman from Gali-
lee whom Christ called to be "a fisher of men" for the Kingdom.

A railing encircles the open oval space and double ramp of
marble stairs that lead to a horseshoe-shaped room. Eighty-six
elegant bronze candle holders line the railing and the stairs. If
you could descend these stairs, you would find yourself face-to-face
with a sumptuous wall and a small recessed sanctuary behind a

richly decorated gilded gate. This is the Niche of the Palliums, so named because wool shorn from baby lambs that the Pope receives in his apartment each year on January 21, the feast of St. Agnes, are woven by nuns into palliums, narrow consecrated strips worn by metropolitan archbishops to represent their authority.

During the pontificate of Pius XII, excavations were conducted under St. Peter's that brought to light a pre-Constantine necropolis, remnants of Constantine's paleo-Christian basilica, including two earlier altars, and the site of Peter's tomb, which, astonishingly enough, was located precisely beneath the main altar of the basilica.

The papal altar itself consists of a bare marble slab found on the site of the Imperial Roman Forum. Bernini's 29-meter-high gilded bronze baldachin over the altar, while immense, nonetheless adds to the sensation of harmony we have felt throughout the basilica.

Above us rises the hallmark of this most famous of basilicas, Michelangelo's wondrous dome. Visible for miles, and especially suggestive when illuminated at night, the dome rests of four colossal piers, rises 120 meters above the floor, and is 42.56 meters wide. Although designed by Michelangelo, it was built by the new basilica's first architect, Donato Bramante. The mosaics on the dome take your breath away, not just by their sheer beauty and craftsmanship, but by the mere thought of how difficult it must have been to execute them (a thought that recurs many times as one visits the church!). They are among the oldest and most valuable in the church. The four large mosaic medallions depict the four Evangelists—Matthew, Mark, Luke and John.

Only the drum of the dome had been finished when Michelangelo died in 1564. Work was interrupted, but resumed in 1588 and, thanks to the work of eight hundred laborers working day and night (by torchlight), was completed in twenty-two months.

A HOLY YEAR IN ROME

We spoke of the piers supporting the dome. In the niches of these piers (facing the apse, going clockwise, starting with the pier in the first column on the right aisle) we see the statues of four saints: Longinus (sculpted by Bernini), Andrew, Veronica, and Helena. Under the pedestal of St. Longinus is the staircase leading down to the Vatican Grottoes. Each statue represents a relic that is preserved in the respective pier: the spearhead with which the Roman centurion Longinus (who converted to Christianity) wounded Christ; the head of St. Andrew, brother of Peter; the veil Veronica used to wipe the face of Jesus as He walked to Calvary; and a piece of the True Cross brought to Rome by Constantine's mother, St. Helena.

Three of these relics—the spear, Veronica's veil, and pieces of the True Cross—are preserved in the Relic Room of the St. Veronica pier. One of the little-known facts about these relics is that they are displayed once a year during Holy Week from the loggia or balcony above St. Veronica's statue. One relic is shown Holy Thursday, a second on Good Friday, and the third on Holy Saturday.

The fourth relic, the head of the Apostle Andrew, was given by Blessed Paul VI to Greek Orthodox Patriarch Athenagoras and is now in Patras, Greece. St. Andrew is the patron saint of the Orthodox. It was St. Andrew, the brother of Simon Peter, who found the five barley loaves and the two fish to give to Jesus to feed the multitudes (John 6:9). Andrew preached in Greece and was crucified in Achaia. He is buried beneath the altar in a chapel below the cathedral of Amalfi, Italy. His feast day is November 30.

Also on the Longinus pier is the world-famous bronze statue of a seated St. Peter, attributed to the thirteenth-century sculptor Arnolfo di Cambio. One of the feet of this much-venerated statue is almost worn away, having been kissed or touched by millions of pilgrims over the centuries. The statue is dressed in pontifical vestments each year on February 22, the feast of the Chair of Peter, and on June 29, the feast of Sts. Peter and Paul, Apostles.

We said at the start that, if architecture is frozen music, then St. Peter's is a symphony. The players are not only those world-renowned artists who created, designed, built, and embellished it, or the Popes who commissioned the work: they are, as well, the tens of millions of pilgrims who, over the centuries, have visited the basilica, to worship or just to tour. In this sense, it is an unfinished symphony.

❖

BASILICA OF ST. JOHN LATERAN

History tells us that Constantine the Great, emperor of the Roman Empire, on the night of October 27, 312, the vigil of the battle of Ponte Milvio in the north of Rome, where he defeated his rival, Emperor Maxentius, had a vision in which he saw a ray of light in the shape of a cross and heard the words "In this sign you shall conquer."

Constantine, who ruled from 306 to 337, not only converted to Christianity but, with the Edict of Milan in 313, granted Christians religious freedom and, as a sign of gratitude for his victory, built one of the world's greatest churches, dedicating it to the Redeemer. He wished the church known today as St. John Lateran to be the greatest, the Mother, of all churches. In fact, the Latin inscription on the principal façade (for the basilica has two façades), commissioned by Pope Clement XII in 1735, reads: "Sacrosancta Lateranensis ecclesia omnium urbis et orbis ecclesiarum mater et caput" (The most holy church of the Lateran, mother and head of all the churches of Rome and of the world).

The same year that he granted religious freedom to Christians, Constantine gave the land and buildings that had belonged to the Roman consular family Laterani—and which had been given to him in dowry by his wife Fausta, the sister of Maxentius—to Pope Melchiades (or Miltiades, an African, and Pope from 311 to 314), who immediately commissioned the courtroom hall of the palaces to be turned into a church.

The original five-nave basilica was consecrated in 314, shortly after Melchiades's death, by his successor, Pope Sylvester I (314-335), who dedicated the church to the Redeemer. It was known as the Constantine Basilica until 1144, when Pope Lucius II (1144-1145) added the names of St. John the Baptist and St. John the Evangelist, and the church became known as St. John Lateran.

In the more than sixteen centuries that have passed since St. John Lateran, the cathedral church of the Pope, the Bishop of Rome, was founded, it has been embellished, damaged by fires and earthquakes, rebuilt, left to languish during the Avignon papacy, and further rebuilt and embellished.

Today the church complex consists of the archbasilica itself, the adjacent Lateran Palace, formerly known as the Patriarchium (home today to the offices of the cardinal vicar of Rome), and the building in which the Lateran Treaty was signed on February 11, 1929, which regulated Church-State relations in Italy, and created the sovereign Vatican City State, the nearby Baptistry, and the building that houses the Scala Santa, or Holy Staircase, and the Sancta Sanctorum, or Holy of Holies. Popes resided at the Patriarchium for nearly a thousand years—until the transfer of the papacy to Avignon in 1309. Upon their return to Rome in

1377, they took up residence a year later in what we know today as the Vatican.

Earlier we spoke of the two façades of St. John Lateran. The north façade is a double portico built by Domenico Fontana and frescoed by artists in the sixteenth century. Here we find the Loggia of Blessings—the gallery from which the Pope blessed the populace. Atop the porticoes are two bell towers dating from the twelfth century, and in the square in front of this entrance is one of the twelve Egyptian obelisks existing in Rome today. This red oriental granite obelisk, commemorating Pharaoh Tutmose III, is the highest in Rome at 47 meters and the oldest, dating from 1500 B.C. It was brought from Thebes to Alexandria, then to the Circus Maximus in Rome in 357. It was placed here by Fontana in 1588 on the order of Pope Sixtus V (1585-1590).

The principal façade, the mammoth east-facing stone one through which most visitors enter the basilica, was, as we said earlier, commissioned by Pope Clement XII in 1735. Visible from miles away are the fifteen colossal travertine statues, each 7 meters high, of Christ the Redeemer, Sts. John the Baptist and John the Evangelist, and twelve Doctors of the Latin and Greek churches, signifying the doctrinal unity of the Church.

There are five entrances in the columned, double-portico outer façade, which in turn opens onto the inner façade and atrium, which has five doors, corresponding to the five naves of the basilica. The mammoth bronze central doors are from the Roman Forum, from the building where the Roman Senate met. They had been transferred in the seventh century to the Church of St. Hadrian in the Forum, and then in 1660 to the basilica by Pope Alexander VII (1655-1667). The furthest door on the right is the Holy Door.

The custom of opening a Holy Door to mark the start of a Jubilee Year began with Pope Martin V (1417-1431), who initiated this practice for the Jubilee Year 1423. The door at St. John Lateran, like all Holy Doors, remains sealed until the start of a Holy Year. This one is sealed with 830 bricks, most of which are given to Church and other dignitaries, when the door is unsealed and opened at the start of a Jubilee. Martin V is buried in the Confessio beneath the papal altar of St. John Lateran.

The interior of this papal basilica, like its principal façade, was planned, as one historian said, "in the great Tuscan manner, combining the colossal with the harmonious." In fact, our senses are assailed as we enter the basilica by the central nave and study the spacious, harmonious, sumptuous beauty that surrounds us, the marvelous Baroque creation of Francesco Borromini.

The central nave itself is 16 meters wide and 87 meters long, the same dimensions as those of St. Mary Major. Welcoming us, on both right and left, are statues of the twelve Apostles, each 4.5 meters high, placed in elaborate niches on massive columns. Above them are twelve stucco bas-reliefs depicting scenes from the Old and New Testaments. Still higher up are twelve medallion oil paintings of the prophets. They were executed during the pontificate of Clement XI (1700-1721) who, it is said, received the twelve artists in audience on the feast of the Ascension in 1718 and made a gift to each of a commemorative medal and 200 scudi.

Our attention is now riveted on the breathtaking gilded wood paneled ceiling, which rises 30 meters above us and was commissioned by the Medici Pope Pius IV (1560-1565). When the sun pours into the basilica through the upper-level windows, especially in late afternoon, the ceiling looks as if it is on fire, and the carvings seem to shimmer in the luminosity.

Back to earth, if you will, the beautiful cosmatesque pavement, restored by Martin V, now captures our attention. (*Cosmatesque* refers to a form of art that derives its name from the stonecutting family Cosma.) We note the repeated use of a column carved into the marble flooring; this was the symbol of Martin's family, the Colonnas.

Following these "columns" as if they were arrows, we arrive at the main, or papal, altar. In ancient times there was a large silver canopy over the altar that contained relics, including part of what was believed to have been the altar used by the first Popes — from St. Peter to St. Sylvester I, the Pontiff who consecrated the first basilica in 314. That relic now rests within the current altar of white marble, built in the last century.

Above the altar, supported by four columns of oriental granite, rises the baldachin, a light and elegant Gothic structure, executed in 1367 on the command of Pope Urban V (1362-1370) and completed with the financial assistance of Charles V of France. The pointed baldachin is decorated with many small statues of saints and with twelve paintings representing scenes in the lives of Jesus, Mary, and several saints. In the uppermost level, behind the grillwork, are two silver busts of Sts. Peter and Paul, said to contain the saints' heads. Beneath the altar, in the confession, is the tomb of Martin V, of the Colonna family.

If our senses have been overwhelmed up to this point, they now come to a standstill as we take in the richness, elegance, and soaring grandeur of the transept and apse.

The splendid luminous setting we see today is the result of the 1597-1601 restoration of the transept. With its breathtaking mosaics, paintings, ornamental ceiling, side chapels, and various tombs (Innocent III and Leo XIII), it is the perfect setting for the papal altar, the stunning Chapel of the Blessed Sacrament, and the monumental Baroque organ executed in 1598 by Luca Blasi of Perugia.

The jewel in this crown is the Blessed Sacrament Chapel, erected by Clement VIII (1592-1605). The tympanum is supported by four gilded columns that, it is said, came from the ships of Cleopatra and, later, from Constantine's palace. The tabernacle is embellished with rare stones of jasper and lapis lazuli. Above the altar is a bas-relief of the Last Supper, behind which is preserved a piece from the table said to be used by Our Lord for the Last Supper, when He instituted the Eucharist.

We move to the center of the transept, to the apse, whose glory practically shouts at the visitor. It was reconstructed between 1878 and 1886, by order of Pope Leo XIII (1878-1903), and its exquisite mosaics focus on the Redeemer. Below the Redeemer, they depict a jeweled cross topped by a dove in the heavens above Jerusalem, and from this the four rivers that empty into the Jordan. The figures on both sides of the Cross are Our Lady, Sts. Peter, Paul, John the Baptist, John the Evangelist, and Andrew. Below them, and between the windows, are nine Apostles, separated by palm trees. Some of the frescoes date from the time of Constantine and the first basilica: these were restored by Franciscans in the thirteenth century. Some of the larger figures, including the Virgin, date from the ninth century. The walnut stalls on both sides of the apse are for the archpriest of the basilica and the twenty-two canons. The throne at the center is used by the Pope when he is at his cathedral church.

In the two side walls of the presbytery are two large frescoes and two immense organs, the latter dating to 1886.

Returning to the entrance of the basilica, we will now discover the treasures of the two side aisles.

Let's start on the right aisle near the Holy Door, where we find the tomb of Paolo Mellini with a fresco of the Madonna and Child. To our right is the Orsini Chapel, designed by Borromini and featuring a fresco of the Conception. Next is the late neoclassic chapel of the Torlonia family, one of the last built for Roman nobility and dedicated to St. John Nepomucene. The altar, with its Russian malachite and lapis lazuli, is quite lovely.

Between these two chapels, on a pillar to our left, is a fragment of a fresco attributed to Giotto, which portrays Pope Boniface VIII proclaiming the very first Jubilee Year, the Holy Year 1300. Next to this is a pillar with a cenotaph (a monument to a deceased person who is buried elsewhere) to Sylvester II, who died in 1003. Legend has it that the monument's inscription to Sylvester II, renown as a magician and astrologer, "sweats" and emits sounds of creaking bones when the death of a Pope is imminent. Also on our left, on the fifth pillar we find the tomb of Pope Sergio IV, who died in 1012 and who saved the Holy Sepulchre of Jerusalem from being destroyed. On the next column is a monument to Alexander II.

Continuing on in the right aisle we come to the chapel of the Massimo family, designed by Giacomo della Porta. Next is an entrance to the adjacent Lateran Palace, mentioned earlier, which is adorned by four pillars of rare red cipolin marble, the four "whispering pillars" where you can hear the echo of your voice if you speak into just one pillar. At the far end of the right aisle—we are now in the right arm of the transept—is the Chapel of the Crucifix with a monument to Cardinal Rezzonico, a fresco depicting the Presentation of Christ in the Temple, and a marble figure of Pope Boniface IX. Still in the transept, and near the presbytery, is the tomb of Innocent III.

To the left of the Chapel of the Crucifix is the entrance to the basilica's museum, opened in 1986 and containing precious works collected by popes, sovereigns, cardinals, and Roman nobility over the centuries. The collection includes precious chalices, processional tintinnabulum (wind chimes or an assemblage of bells), a thirteenth-century station cross, tapestries, and monstrances.

A HOLY YEAR IN ROME

Crossing over to the left aisle, and working our way from the apse-transept area to the main entrance, we find in the left arm of the transept the tomb of Leo XIII. On the adjacent wall is a bejeweled cross that was given by Roman nobility to the basilica in commemoration of the Holy Year 1900. Moving on, we immediately find the Chapel of the Colonna family, on whose vault there is a fresco portraying the Coronation of Mary. Four rare pink alabaster columns surround the altar, above which is a work by Cavalier D'Arpino, the *Saviour*. To the altar's left is the tomb of Lucrezia Tomacelli, the wife of Filippo Colonna.

As we proceed down the left aisle, toward the basilica entrance, we now come to the Chapel of the Sacrament, which we described earlier in some detail, as well as the entrance to the cloister. Beyond this chapel is the Chapel of the Mauri family of Parma. Next is the Lancellotti Chapel, dedicated to St. Francis of Assisi, designed by Francesco de Volterra in 1588. We now come to the Onorio Longhi Chapel, commemorating the papal soldiers who fell in the war of 1860. The last chapel in this aisle, before we leave the basilica, is the elegant eighteenth-century chapel of the Corsini family, in the shape of a Greek cross and built above an ancient cemetery. This is where the Pope, whose cathedral church this is, vests when he celebrates Mass here.

A visit to St. John Lateran, a church that encompasses almost the entire history of Christianity, should, in truth, be a prolonged visit, one that gives the pilgrim time to visit every inch of this splendid basilica, to wander in the peaceful adjacent cloisters and to see the Baptistry (one of whose chapels has a wooden ceiling designed by Michelangelo in 1500) and the museum.

However, we cannot take our leave without mentioning the Scala Santa, or Holy Stairs. Well-documented tradition has it that the twenty-eight steps on which Jesus walked in Pilate's house in

Jerusalem were brought to Rome by Constantine's mother, St. Helena , who was responsible for bringing to Rome relics, including part of the True Cross, a nail that pierced Our Lord, and Veronica's veil.

Today these marble-covered steps, which can be ascended only on one's knees, are housed across from the basilica in a building constructed by Domenico Fontana, who worked on this at the same time he was building the northern portico of the basilica. The Scala Santa lead to what used to be the private chapel of the Popes, the Oratory of St. Lawrence, and what is now called the Sancta Sanctorum (Holy of Holies), so named for the great number of relics it used to house. Behind a grillwork lies the chapel, over whose altar is a picture of the Redeemer called the *Acheropita*—that is, not painted by human hands—a sixth-century icon much revered by Romans. Above the altar is the inscription: "Non est in toto sanctior orbe locus" ("There is no holier place in the world than this").

Two staircases running parallel to the Holy Stairs allow visitors to ascend and descend on foot.

Outside, on part of the building that used to house the dining room of the Papal Palace, is a great apse containing a ninth-century mosaic, restored in 1743 and again in 1933.

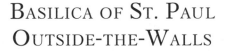

BASILICA OF ST. PAUL OUTSIDE-THE-WALLS

St. Paul Outside-the-Walls, the second largest church in Rome after St. Peter's Basilica, stands on the burial place of the Apostle on Rome's Via Ostiense, about two kilometers outside the

A HOLY YEAR IN ROME

Aurelian walls near the left bank of the Tiber. As burials were not allowed within city walls, the church built to commemorate St. Paul was located outside the city, thus the name St. Paul Outside-the-Walls.

Construction on the original church began during the reign of the first Christian emperor, Constantine (306-337), who was also responsible for the building of St. John Lateran and St. Peter's. In fact, it is said that St. Paul's and the original St. Peter's were consecrated on the same day—November 18, 324. Constantine, it is written, wished to memorialize St. Paul, whose body, after he was decapitated, was taken by a Roman Christian, Lucina, for burial in a small graveyard adjacent to Via Ostiense, in an area called *ad acquas salvias* (saving waters).

Today this former cemetery is the site of a Trappist monastery known as Le Tre Fontane, "the Three Fountains." Legend has it that when St. Paul was beheaded, his severed head hit the ground three times, and in each of the places it touched the ground, a fountain sprang up; thus, the name Le Tre Fontane.

In 380, Pope Damasus asked the three coreigning emperors, Valentinian II, Theodosius, and Arcadian, to build a new place of worship over the Constantinian basilica. Construction on the "basilica of the three emperors" began between 384 and 386. The first disaster, an earthquake, struck in 441, and Pope Leo the Great (440-461) undertook the rebuilding.

What we see today is the result of building and rebuilding as the basilica, over the centuries, was the victim of several catastrophic fires and earthquakes, as well as sacking by the Lombards and the Saracens. The present edifice is the result of more than a century of work that began after the last disastrous fire, in 1823, which devastated the church. Among the items saved from that fire, and still seen today, were the Gothic-style tabernacle executed at the end of the thirteenth century by Arnolfo di Cambio, and the 5-meter-high Easter candlestick, sculpted by Pietro Vassalletto and Niccolo D'Angelo in 1170, believed to be the oldest, tallest, and most precious in the world.

What first strikes the visitor upon arrival at the basilica is the great sense of peace. It is surrounded by trees and parks, and offers a relative oasis of tranquillity from city chaos.

Before we go to the west side of this complex, to the main entrance, we should stop a minute on the east side to observe the 65-meter-high bell tower. Built between 1840 and 1860 by Luigi Poletti, the tower is divided into five stories and is completely covered in travertine. The top floor resembles a small Roman temple. It has sixteen Corinthian columns and a high spherical vault, topped by the cross and orb, and can be reached by a spiral travertine staircase with 296 steps. Seven bells hang in the top three floors, four of which came from the previous basilica.

Built within an immense four-sided portico, the basilica complex seems an island unto itself. Access to the majestic porticoed atrium, with its garden, palm trees, and monumental statue of St. Paul, is through the west wall with its thirteen arches, which contain paintings depicting Christ and the Apostles. The north and south walls of the atrium are each 70 meters long, and the entire area is flanked by 150 columns, arranged in single file at the basilica entrance, double on the north and south walls, and triple on the west side.

Standing in the portico, our attention is riveted to the upper part of the façade, with its spectacular mosaics produced between 1854 and 1874 by the Vatican Mosaic Laboratory. They depict the prophets Isaiah, Jeremiah, Ezekiel, and Daniel, above whom are the *agnus dei*, the lambs of God, and on the topmost level, Christ giving His blessing to Sts. Peter and Paul.

A HOLY YEAR IN ROME

There are five entrances to the church itself, although the central one, or Bronze Door, and the one to its right, the Holy Door, are usually closed. The Holy Door, as we know, is open only during a Holy Year.

The mammoth Bronze Door — 7.48 meters high and 3.35 meters wide — was made between 1929 and 1931 by the sculptor Antonio Maraini. It consists of twelve panels, dominated by a cross of vine shoots of silver damascene, interspersed by ovals of lapis lazuli on which are figured the busts of the Apostles. The figure of Christ, executed in silver, is the focal point of each of the third panels from the bottom. These panels represent an important moment in the lives of Sts. Peter and Paul in their relation to Christ: the handing of the keys to St. Peter and the conversion of St. Paul.

The interior of St. Paul Outside-the Walls is breathtaking in its splendor, size, and classical beauty. In the shape of a Latin cross, it is divided into five naves, marked by four rows of twenty columns each. Larger than a football field, it is 131 meters long, 65 meters wide, and 30 meters high. The counter-façade is decorated by six alabaster columns donated by the Egyptian viceroy Muhammad Ali in 1840.

If there is one drawback to this stunning church, it is a relative lack of light, even on the sunniest of days. Greater light would allow the visitor to appreciate better the breadth, depth, and symmetry of the church, with its eighty columns; the ten statues of the Apostles in as many niches on the sides of the outermost naves; the floor, which seems like a marble carpet; the wonderful carving of the gilded coffered ceiling, which depicts the coats of arms of the various popes linked with the building of the basilica; and the upper-level windows and thirty-six frescoes depicting scenes from the life of St. Paul.

Also relatively obscured is the splendid Byzantine Door, which is now the inner side of the Holy Door, but which used to be the main entrance to the basilica before the 1823 fire. From Latin and Greek inscriptions on the door, we know it was produced in 1070 by an artist named Teodoro.

The relative lack of light also obscures what has perhaps become the "trademark" feature of this basilica, the series of mosaic portraits of all the popes—from St. Peter to Pope Francis, the 266th successor to St. Peter.

The so-called Papal Portraits are to be found above the columns in the naves and in the transept. The first series of frescoed portraits was begun by Pope Leo the Great. Only forty-one remained after the great fire of 1823, and they are now in the basilica museum. In May 1847 Pius IX (1846-1878) ordered a new series of portraits, to be done this time in mosaics, assigning the work to the Vatican Mosaic Laboratory.

Legend has it that when the last papal portrait is done, the world will end. With the mosaic of Pope Francis, there are now eleven blank medallions for the portraits of future Pontiffs. All current Pontiffs are literally "spotlighted" so that the mosaic portrait of each stands out.

St. Paul's has, perhaps, the most glorious mosaics of all the basilicas. And their greatest glory can be found in the triumphal arch and the apse. At the center of the triumphal arch, the entryway to the apse and the main altar is Christ between two angels and the twenty-four men of the Apocalypse, giving His blessing. On the right and left sides of the lower half, below each group of twelve men, are the figures of Sts. Peter and Paul. The apse features Christ on His throne in the center, with Sts. Peter and Andrew on His left, and Sts. Paul and Luke on His right. The panel below contains a representation of the Hetimasia (the empty throne with the Cross and instruments of martyrdom) between two angels and twelve figures of Apostles and saints.

The new basilica was dedicated by Pius IX on December 10, 1854, two days after he proclaimed the dogma of the Immaculate Conception in the constitution *Ineffabilis Deus*. On the walls of the semicircular apse, below the mosaics we have just described, are memorial tablets with the names of all those who participated in this momentous event: the complete College of Cardinals, the patriarch of Alexandria, and 140 bishops.

The radiant mosaics act as a frame to the main altar and to the most sacred part of the church—why it was built and why we are here—the Confession, the burial place of St. Paul the Apostle. Ringed by a white marble balustrade, a double staircase leads to the tomb, just below the papal altar. Beyond the altar grillwork, one can look down and see a slab bearing the inscription *"Paulo Apostolo Mart,"* said to date from the fifth century. A marble porphyry within the altar contains the remains of St. Timothy.

Rising above the papal altar and the tomb of the Apostle is the splendid Gothic canopy or tabernacle executed by Arnolfo di Cambio, which is supported by four porphyry columns.

As we explore the transept of the basilica, we note the two identical altars placed on the north and south sides. On our right, the south side, is the Altar of the Assumption, and on our left, the Conversion of St. Paul. The two altar tables are encrusted with malachite, donated by Czar Nicholas I, and with lapis lazuli. There are four chapels on the eastern wall of the transept. From left to right: St. Stephen's Chapel, the Chapel of the Blessed Sacrament, St. Lawrence's Chapel, and St. Benedict's Chapel.

Doors on either side of the Altar of the Assumption bring us to both the Baptistry and the Oratory of St. Julian. The Baptistry was built in 1930, using part of the earlier basilica. The frescoes, for example, can be dated to 1460. The walls and floor are polychromatic marble. The baptismal font is decorated with malachite, lapis lazuli, and mother of pearl.

The Oratory of St. Julian, now used as a bookstore, links the basilica to one of the loveliest parts of the entire church complex, the thirteenth-century cloister. The cloister is also adjacent to a Benedictine monastery, the order that has been the custodian of this basilica for centuries.

Often called the most beautiful cloister in Rome, this one is a marvel of cosmatesque art. The rectangular garden, whose cross-shaped walkways divide the shrub-bordered lawn and flowerbeds into four equal parts, with a fountain in the center, is framed by a four-sided ambulatory. Gracious arches and small, coupled columns—some smooth, others fluted, spiraling, or twisted—lend an air of overall delicacy to the cloister. The mosaic-covered lintels and richly sculpted cornice add to the well-balanced beauty and serenity. The ambulatory walls are embedded with lapidaries spanning the centuries. There is also a richly decorated sarcophagus and a statue of Pope Boniface, dating from the end of the fourteenth century.

BASILICA OF ST. MARY MAJOR

The year was 358. John, a Roman patrician, and his wife, unable to have children, had been praying faithfully to the Virgin, asking her to give them a sign as to whom they should leave their enormous patrimony to. The night of August 4, one of the hottest of the year, Mary appeared to the couple in a dream and requested that they build a church in her honor where snow would fall that night.

John and his wife went to tell Pope Liberius of their dream and, to their amazement, discovered that the Pontiff had had the same dream. On the morning of August 5, the highest of Rome's seven fabled hills, the Esquiline, was covered in snow, as witnessed by John, his wife, the Pope and his entourage, and a throng of Romans. Pope Liberius took a stick and traced the sign of the future basilica in the snow, a basilica that would be forever known as Our Lady of the Snows, in addition to the name it bears today, St. Mary Major, the greatest—and the oldest—Marian church.

The feast of Our Lady of the Snows was introduced that year and has been commemorated ever since on August 5. Each year, during vespers, thousands of white flower petals, symbolizing the miraculous snowfall, are released from the basilica's rooftop, both inside and outside, showering the faithful who have gathered to commemorate that event.

St. Mary Major, one of the seven major basilicas of Rome, is also one of the four papal basilicas (the others being St. Peter's, St. John Lateran, and St. Paul Outside-the-Walls) that must be visited by pilgrims in a Holy Year to obtain an indulgence.

Also known as the Liberian Basilica (for Pope Liberius), the first church of St. Mary Major was originally built on the site of an ancient market and close to the Temple of Juno Lucina. Over the centuries, it underwent changes, modifications, and additions. Excavations carried out under Pope Paul VI (1963-1978) revealed the remains of a first-century Roman building and a porticoed courtyard containing many second- and third-century frescoes and decorations.

Much of the basilica that we see today is due to Pope Sixtus III (432-440). Sixtus became Pope one year after the Ecumenical

Council of Ephesus (in modern-day Turkey), which recognized Mary as *Theotokos*, the Mother of God. This third ecumenical council, convened to fight the heresies of Nestorianism and Pelagianism, defined the Hypostatic Union of the divine and human natures in the one Person of Christ. Thus Mary, Mother of the man Jesus, was also Mother of God.

Pope Sixtus wished to honor this, the most noble, of all of the Blessed Virgin's titles. It was he who gave the basilica much of its current structure and form, as well as the magnificent mosaics on the Ephesus Triumphal Arch, which is above and behind the main altar and which depicts scenes from the New Testament.

St. Mary Major today is a canticle to the most blessed of all women, to Theotokos, to the titles that have been conferred on her in the Litany of the Blessed Virgin: Mother of the Church, Mother of Divine Grace, Mother Most Chaste, Mother of Our Creator, Mystical Rose, Tower of David, Sanctuary of the Divine, Help of Christians, and Queen of Angels, to name but a few of the many titles in the litany.

It is a hymn of love to the Mother of God, a hymn sung over the centuries by the painters, gold- and silversmiths, woodworkers, sculptors, mosaic artists, and even simple laborers—the unknown artisans who carved the niches and monumental pillars and who laid the intricate marble floor—who worked to create this magnificent temple.

We start our visit on the square in front of the south-facing façade of the basilica, where there is a column from the basilica of Maxentius in the Roman Forum, the only intact pillar from that temple. Pope Paul V (1605-1621) ordered the 14-meter column brought to St. Mary Major in 1613: a year later, the bronze statue of Madonna and Child, with Mary's foot resting on the moon, was set atop the column.

A HOLY YEAR IN ROME

On the northern side of the basilica is a 14-meter-high obelisk, built by the Emperor Diocletian (A.D. 96) with Egyptian materials. It once stood outside the mausoleum of Augustus but was resurrected by Domenico Fontana and brought to St. Mary Major on the orders of Pope Sixtus V, whose coat of arms tops the obelisk.

As we turn now to gaze at the façade of the basilica, we are drawn by two astonishing works: the three-arched loggia, part of the ancient front of the church dating from 1290, with its stunning mosaics portraying the miracle of the snow, and the 75-meter-high Romanesque campanile or bell tower, the highest in Rome. Rising six stories, it was commissioned by Gregory XI (1370-1378) in 1377, upon the return of the papacy from its exile in Avignon, France.

The current façade was built in 1761 by Ferdinando Fuga. Five grillwork openings bring us to the atrium. In the center is the great Bronze Door, first commissioned by Pope Pius XI (1922-1939) and completed in time for the 1950 Holy Year. To the far left of the Bronze Door is the Holy Door, first consecrated for the Jubilee Year 1500.

Once inside the basilica, the third most visited monument in Rome after St. Peter's and the Coliseum, we are struck by both its size and the harmony it projects, notwithstanding the myriad architectural changes it has undergone in the past fifteen hundred years.

The central nave is as high as it is wide—16 meters—is 86.5 meters long, and is flanked by forty ancient Roman monolithic columns, four granite and thirty-six Ionic ones of marble. The two side aisles are ten meters wide each. The so-called cosmatesque pavement was executed by the marble workers of the Cosmati guild in 1288 and was the gift of two Roman nobles, Scoto and Giovanni Paparoni, relatives of the archpriest of the basilica, Orlando Paparoni. The remains of the patrician John and his wife, who paid for the first basilica in the fourth century, are interred under the fifth large granite circle in the central aisle.

Before taking another step, however, we pause to contemplate the arrestingly beautiful ceiling, commissioned by Pope Alexander VI (1492-1503) for the Holy Year 1500 and designed by Giuliano da Sangallo. It consists of 105 wood-carved panels, each a meter square, which were placed over the former trussed ceiling and then gilded with some of the gold brought from the newly discovered Americas by Columbus and given to King Ferdinand and Queen Isabella of Spain. The Peruvian gold was then donated by the Spanish Royals to Pope Alexander VI, also a Spaniard. This added magnificence induced Romans to call this "the golden basilica."

The basilica has been under the patronage of Spanish kings since that time, and even today the Spanish monarch is a canon of St. Mary Major. In theory, the king should visit the basilica once a year. If he cannot do so, he names a delegate, usually the Spanish Ambassador to the Holy See. Once every year, there is a Mass in the basilica for Spain and the Spanish people.

Twenty-four canons, named by the Holy Father, are responsible for the basilica—for its administration, repairs, and the day-to-day tasks of overseeing visitors and preparing liturgical services. Their tasks in recent years have included preparing a full calendar of events for Jubilee Years when they occur.

Before we explore the two side aisles with their striking chapels, side altars, tombs, and statues, we will go to the front of the Church, to four focal points: the imposing main altar and baldachin, framed by the exquisite Ephesus Triumphal Arch, which we mentioned earlier, the Sistine or Sacrament Chapel, the Borghese or Pauline Chapel and the Confession, below the main altar with the monument to Pius IX (1846-1878), and the relics of the Sacred Crib.

A HOLY YEAR IN ROME

The Triumphal Arch of Ephesus forms a rich and elegant gateway to the apse, main altar, and transept. Pope Sixtus III, we said, commissioned this arch in 431, a year after Mary was proclaimed Mother of God at the Council of Ephesus. The incomparably beautiful and exquisitely detailed mosaics, incorporating 190 types of enamels and colors, depict nine events relative to Jesus, Mary, and the Holy Family. For some inexplicable reason, they are not in chronological order as you study them, going in a clockwise direction from the lower left.

Nonetheless, starting from the lower left, and ending on the lower right, we have: Jerusalem, where Jesus died; Herod ordering all male children under the age of two to be killed; the Divine Child on a throne, protected by Mary and four angels and adored by the Magi; the Annunciation; a circle inside of which is the Throne of God, with a crown, a royal mantle, and on the stool the book of the Apocalypse and the New Law; the Presentation in the Temple; the Holy Family arriving in Egypt after their flight; the Magi asking Herod where to find the "new King of the Jews"; and Bethlehem, where Jesus was born.

Below the triumphal arch is the main altar that lies beneath a sculpted wood baldachin designed by Fuga and is supported by four porphyry columns from the ancient portico. The sarcophagus that is the base of the altar dates from 1749 and contains the relics of St. Matthias the Apostle (chosen to take the place of Judas Iscariot), Semplicius, Faustinus, and Beatrice, which had been venerated from the thirteenth century in a reliquary elsewhere in the church. In addition it contains the remains of St. Jerome, which had been kept in a marble urn under the ancient altar. Two stones containing the relics of St. Stephen the protomartyr and St. Lawrence the deacon were placed on the altar when it was consecrated on September 30, 1750.

Beneath the main altar is the pièce de résistance of St. Mary Major, and for pilgrims the most sacred part of their visit—the Confession and Altar of the Sacred Crib. A horseshoe-shaped double staircase leads to a small chapel that houses the relics of the manger crib in which the Christ Child was laid the night he was born. The crystal, silver, and gold reliquary containing the wood remnants was executed by Valadier in 1802 on the commission of Pope Pius VII (1800-1823), who intended it to be in place for the Holy Year 1825. It replaces two previous reliquaries, the first of which was stolen in 1527, during the Sack of Rome, and the second in 1797 by Napoleon's troops. The altar and Confession are decorated with seventy-four types of precious marble. Five votive lamps hang in the center; a sixth was donated by Ortho-dox Patriarch Athenagoras in 1967. A mammoth statue of Pius IX, kneeling in prayer before the reliquary, greets visitors as they descend into the Confession.

To the right of the main altar, just below the Communion rail (and very easy to miss), is an extremely simple stone that says, "Gian Lorenzo Bernini, glory of the arts and the city, humbly lies here." Bernini, as we have seen, was a sculptor, architect and painter, and one of the Renaissance's most brilliant sons.

And now it is time to visit the two most stupendous chapels of the basilica, which beckon by the brilliance of their art as well as by the light entering from their domed ceilings. At one point, the entire basilica was much more luminous, but half of the clerestory windows have been walled up, thus closing out much of the natural light. You might have noticed this relative lack of light in all the basilicas you have visited, as there is little lighting, natural or man-made, during the day. The full and breathtaking magnificence of all of these churches, however, can be seen during a liturgical function when they are brilliantly lit. This is when every statue, pillar, column, bas-relief, painting, mosaic, altar canopy, candelabra, and reliquary can be seen in its most minute detail and in all its splendor.

At the end of the right aisle is the Chapel of the Sacrament, or Sistine Chapel (not to be confused with the one painted by Michelangelo in the Vatican), which was commissioned by Sixtus V (1585-1590) shortly before he became Pope, when he was still Cardinal of Montalto. Executed by Domenico Fontana, this chapel was originally intended to house the ancient Oratory of the Crib to which the Pontiff was devoted. Its radiantly beautiful cupola depicts the life of the Virgin, the infancy of Jesus, and the nine orders of angels. Frescoes, small side altars, and statues of Sts. Peter, Bishop of Alexandria, Dominic, Francis of Assisi, Anthony of Padua, and Peter and Paul all draw our attention, but the centerpiece is the main and papal altar, which has a temple-like tabernacle baldachin in gilded bronze which reproduces the chapel itself.

St. Mary Major has the singular honor of being the only church in the world to have two papal altars: the main altar we saw earlier, which contains the relics of the Apostles, and this altar in the Chapel of the Sacrament.

The steps at the *Confessio* in front of the altar lead to the Oratory of the Crib, where three Popes are buried. Here we find the Grotto of Bethlehem, commissioned by Pope Innocent III in 1198. It was transferred here from a vineyard next to the basilica by Pope Sixtus V, the Pontiff whose name will live forever in the annals of Church art for the sheer amount of works that he ordered to be built or restored. The Madonna and Child is by Valsoldo, and the Three Kings, donkey, and ox are by Arnolfo di Cambio. The Oratory is not always open to visitors, so ask an attendant or sacristan if you can visit.

Just across the way, at the end of the left aisle, is the Pauline or Borghese Chapel, commissioned by Pope Paul V, a member of the

Borghese family, in 1613. It was also he who ordered the building of the major sacristy that we will see shortly in the right aisle.

The Borghese Chapel houses the most beloved of the Marian images venerated in Rome, the *Salus Populi Romani*, or "salvation of the Roman people," as Mary was credited by the Romans for sparing them from the plague in 1527. The Byzantine-style icon is attributed to St. Luke, and it has been said that Mary herself posed for the original that was venerated in Byzantium. On special occasions it is still carried through the streets of Rome in procession.

In the dome we see the Assumption of the Blessed Virgin Mary, resting her feet on the moon as Galileo saw her through a telescope. Six statues decorate as many niches—St. John the Evangelist, St. Joseph, Aaron, David, St. Bernard, and Denis Aereopagitus. On the side walls are the tomb of Clement VIII and a monument to Paul V. There are perhaps entire churches elsewhere in Rome (or the world) that are not decorated as sumptuously as is this chapel with its finely sculpted statues and bas-reliefs; the strikingly rich variety of marble used in the pillars, on the altars, and the floor; the vibrant frescoes; the elegant candelabra; and the gold which seems to be everywhere. In a word, it is breathtaking.

If we can tear ourselves away from these chapels, we'll study the forty-four mosaics on the left and right sides of the central nave and in the transept-apse area, a true kaleidoscope of color every bit as stunning as those of the triumphal arch in their brilliance, breadth, and scope. A visitor truly wishes to be able to climb a staircase and examine each one up close.

A number of these fifth-century mosaics in the central nave, ordered by Pope Sixtus III, have been lost, but some of these have been reproduced in frescoes. Featuring scenes of major events and people from the Old Testament, such as Noah's Ark or Moses receiving the Ten Commandments, the mosaics are resplendent in their detail and color. At times you expect people to move or speak, trees to sway, water to flow and birds to fly.

The grand and lustrous mosaics of the apse, completed over eight hundred years later, in 1295, were entrusted by Pope Nicholas IV to Franciscan friar Giacomo Torriti. Most represent scenes from the life of Mary, from the Annunciation to the Dormition of Mary, while others depict Sts. Francis of Assisi, Peter and Paul, Anthony of Padua, John the Evangelist, and John the Baptist. Also depicted are Nicholas IV, who commissioned the mosaic, and Cardinal Giacomo Colonna, who donated it.

A series of altars and monuments decorate the right and left aisles of the basilica. Returning to the entrance and starting up the left aisle we see the ornate Cesi Chapel, followed by an altar dedicated to St. Leo and the Virgin Mary, the marble group titled *Regina Pacis* (Queen of Peace) and the altar of St. Francis of Assisi. The next chapel we see is the elaborate Sforza Chapel. The last one on our left is the Borghese or Pauline Chapel, which we have just visited.

We will now go up the right aisle, starting again near the entrance. The first chapel on our right is the Baptistry. Inside, on the right, is the entrance to the beautiful Sacristy of the Canons, a masterpiece by Ponzio, whose vault is decorated with the Coronation of Mary.

Continuing in the right aisle, we see a series of altars and monuments. The first is the Altar of the Holy Family, and then one dedicated to Blessed Albergati. This is followed by the Chapel of the Reliquaries with its ten porphyry columns; behind the grating are reliquaries containing relics of various saints. The next altar we see in the aisle is the Altar of the Annunciation. The last chapel on our right is the Sistine Chapel, which we visited in detail.

We've touched upon only a small portion of the treasures offered by this temple to the Mother of God. There are fifteen hundred years of Church history encompassed in this basilica, and its artwork tells not only that history, but the entire history of salvation — Old Testament and New — from the Annunciation to the birth, life, Crucifixion, death, and Resurrection of Christ, to the Dormition and Assumption of the Blessed Virgin Mary.

BASILICA OF ST. LAWRENCE-OUTSIDE-THE-WALLS

We now visit the fifth of the seven basilicas that comprise our pilgrimage in the Eternal City — the papal basilica of St. Lawrence Outside-the-Walls. This visit is a "two for one" treat, as we will actually see two basilicas. In the previous churches we visited, we noted that construction had begun in the fourth century under Emperor Constantine (except for St. Mary Major, which postdates Constantine). We also noted that additions and renovations over ensuing centuries had changed the appearance, leaving little or none of the original church.

St. Lawrence Outside-the-Walls, however, is a rather noteworthy exception to this, as we find not only parts of the original Constantinian basilica, but the basilica built by Pope Pelagius II (579-590) as well as the basilica added on to that of Pelagius by Pope Honorius III (1216-1227). And this notwithstanding the grave damage done to the basilica during the July 1943 bombing and the subsequent restoration.

A HOLY YEAR IN ROME

Once again Constantine is the main protagonist of our story, which focuses on St. Lawrence, a deacon of the Church who was burned alive on August 10, 258, during the persecutions that also cost Pope Sixtus II his life. A cult had arisen around St. Lawrence, and Emperor Constantine was one of the biggest devotees. In fact, the emperor had isolated the tomb of St. Lawrence, which had been sumptuously embellished in the years following his death, surrounded it with silver grating and constructed an apse to protect it. In 330, to commemorate the saint, he built a basilica, autonomous from the cemetery.

St. Lawrence's tomb was originally in an area known as "*ager Veranus*," land owned by one Lucius Verus that was near the Via Tiburtina and adjacent to Christian cemeteries and catacombs. Today the church is also known as St. Lawrence at Verano.

In the sixth century, Pope Pelagius noted the sorry state of the Constantinian basilica due to the infiltration of water and decided to build a new church, independent of Constantine's and over the tomb of the saint. He added the remains of St. Stephen, which he had brought from Byzantium, to those of St. Lawrence.

Much material from imperial Rome was used in building Pelagius's basilica, principally the pillars, columns, capitals, and balustrades that we still see today and that comprise the sanctuary of the actual basilica. This Pelagian basilica consisted of a nave and two aisles and, to render it more luminous, a series of arched windows were added on the ground level, the second story and the upper level. The second story was known as the *matronei* and was reserved for women only, as was the custom at the time.

In medieval times a small fortified city—known as Laurenzio-poli (Lawrenceopolis)—had arisen around the basilica to protect it from the barbarians (it has already been sacked and plundered by the Vandals and Lombards), complete with high protective walls and defense towers. All that remains today are parts of the wall, a guard tower (now used as a burial place by the Capuchin friars who have been the basilica's custodians since 1855), the bell tower, and the wonderful cloister.

In the thirteenth century, Pope Honorius III undertook a grandiose project to expand and embellish the basilica. He demolished the apse of the Pelagian church (it had no transept), but he kept everything else intact, including the famous and strikingly beautiful triumphal arch (which we have seen throughout our visits to Rome's basilicas). He then proceeded to build the new church out and away from the first one, starting at the triumphal arch. The two basilicas are thus joined, like Siamese twins, so to speak, at the triumphal arch. So today, when we enter the basilica, we are in the church built by Honorius. We proceed up the center aisle to a point where there are steps—directly below the triumphal arch—and, once we ascend these steps, we are in the Pelagian basilica.

But let's back up a bit and start our visit on the gracious piazza in front of the basilica. As we look at the basilica, we note part of the former walls of the fortified city, the twelfth-century eight-story bell tower to the right of the church, and countless tall Italian cypress that are today part of Verano municipal cemetery. In the center of the square is a monument topped by a statue of St. Lawrence and built in memory of the work done on this basilica by Pope Pius IX, whose pontificate of 31 years, 7 months, and 17 days was the second longest in Church history, following that of St. Peter. Pius IX is buried in the basilica. On your right, and behind you, is a statue of Pope Pius XII, commemorating his visit to the basilica on July 19, 1943, immediately following the bombing that same day of the basilica, bombing that heavily damaged the façade and that central nave.

A HOLY YEAR IN ROME

Entering the atrium, we are struck by the forty-eight frescoed panels that decorate the three walls. Dating from the second half of the thirteenth century and restored under Pius IX, they narrate mostly episodes related to the life and death of St. Lawrence, as well as a number from the life of Emperor Henry II, such as the apparition of St. George to the emperor as he leaves for a war with the Slavs. There are also fourteen scenes relative to the life and death of St. Stephen, including the arrival of his relics at St. Lawrence Basilica, and six episodes from the pontificate of Alexander II (1061-1073).

There are several sarcophagi in the atrium, as well as the tomb of Alcide De Gasperi, an Italian statesman who died in 1954. A memorial stone, erected by the faithful in gratitude for Pius XII's July 1943 visit, and placed next to the door on the far right, calls the Pontiff "the angelic pastor."

Once we enter the basilica, we are awed by both its antiquity and the powerful harmony it projects, the stunning oneness of the two basilicas built so many centuries apart. More than any other church we have seen, we are propelled into the past, as if a sacred time machine has been at work. Except for an electric light here and there, it is as if we have traveled centuries back in time.

Stand for a minute to take it all in: the simplicity of the central nave and the eleven columns of diverse widths that separate the nave from the two side aisles, the two side chapels, several funeral monuments, and the wood-beamed ceiling. Walk slowly over the glorious mosaic and marble floor, with its thousand and one ornate designs and large porphyry disks, proceeding past the two stupendous pulpits used for the reading of the Epistle and the Gospel, through the church built by Honorius, until we come to the stairs—below the triumphal arch—which lead us up to the sanctuary and into the Pelagian basilica.

The Seven Pilgrimage Basilicas

Before we move into the sanctuary, however, a closer look at the two thirteenth-century pulpits in the basilica of Honorius and at the triumphal arch is obligatory.

The massive marble and stone pulpit on the left, on a base of Greek and Carrara marble, and decorated with gray marble and porphyry, was used to read the Epistle. The even-more-massive and ornate pulpit on the right, on a base of Greek marble and black-and-white Egyptian granite, also decorated in porphyry, bears a sculpted eagle just under the spot from which the Gospel was read. To the left of the top step of this pulpit is the magnificent candelabra for the Easter candle. In early Christian basilicas, raised platforms known as ambones were built for reading the Epistle and the Gospel. The word comes from the Greek *ambo*, meaning "rim, edge or pulpit."

Now we turn our attention to the majestic triumphal arch, a masterpiece of mosaic work from the sixth century on the side of the Pelagian basilica, and an equally stunning fresco on the Honorius side of the basilica.

The frescoed side of the arch depicts Mary between Sts. Lawrence and Justin on the left and Sts. Stephen and Ciriaca on the right. The prophets Isaiah and Daniel are in the lower portion.

Moving to the Pelagian basilica, we now view the other side of the arch, with its vibrant sixth-century mosaics, as brilliant after all these years as if they had been done yesterday. Christ is at the center, and behind Him is a blue globe. On Christ's right, our left as we view the mosaic, are Pope Pelagius, bearing a replica of the basilica that he is offering to Christ, and Sts. Lawrence and Peter. To Christ's left are Sts. Paul, Stephen, and Hippolytus, the latter bearing the crown of a martyr. In the lower left of the arch is the holy city of Jerusalem, and on the lower right, Bethlehem.

Remaining in the sanctuary, we see that, although a newer altar has been built on the lower level of the basilica, the papal altar, dating from 1148 and covered by a multitiered, columned ciborium or baldachin, is on the raised portion, the basilica built by Pope Pelagius. Behind this altar is the sumptuous and monumental cathedra, or bishop's throne, of stone, marble, gold mosaics, lapis lazuli, and porphyry. This dates from the thirteenth century.

Behind the newer altar, and between the double set of seven steps leading to the upper level and altar, are eight stairs leading down to the crypt or *Confessio* where Sts. Lawrence, Stephen, and Justin are buried. Behind a small marble altar, and within a four-sided, cage-like gilded grating, is a huge marble monument with the remains of the saints. Encased in the center wall is a marble slab on which, it is said, can be seen the outline of the body of St. Lawrence, which had been placed there, still warm, immediately after his death. Eight antique columns of green and white marble surround the tomb and support the ceiling of the crypt. The tomb lies just below the main papal altar, which, we have seen, is in the Pelagian church.

Returning now to the lower basilica of Honorius, we go to the far end of the left nave, where we see the highly decorative entrance to the Chapel of St. Ciriaca, reached by descending a stairway whose curved ceiling and side walls are decorated with marble. The white marble altar dates to the fifteenth century and the papacy of Nicholas V (1447-1455). According to legend, St. Lawrence appeared to a monk and told him that, for every Mass celebrated at this altar, a soul would enter Heaven. A door on one of the side walls leads to the adjacent underground catacombs of St. Ciriaca. Access today, however, is only though the cloister.

Now let's cross over to the right nave. At the far end, just beyond the small Chapel of St. Tarcisius, formerly a sacristy, we arrive at a massive metal gate that leads to the chapel and tomb of Pius IX. It was the wish of Pope Pius IX to be buried in this basilica, in the most simple and humble of tombs and as close as possible to the saint to whom he was so devoted.

The place he chose was the relatively modest and unadorned narthex (an enclosed passage between the main entrance and the nave of a church) of the Pelagian basilica. However, Catholics from Rome and around the world felt he should be remembered in grandeur—and grandeur it was to be. The senses swim with the brilliance of the mosaics, precious stones, and metals that now cover every square inch of the chapel, except for the marble columns and the marble balustrade set into the walls. Ruby reds, fiery golds, aquas, and glittering greens dazzle us as we study the floral designs, Biblical scenes, coats of arms of the various nobility, and insignia of the many religious institutes whose donations made this all possible. A simple black wrought-iron grille has been erected in front of the Pontiff's tomb, just across from the chapel entrance.

Five mosaics on the entrance wall are worthy of note: the medallions depicting St. Alphonsus de Liguori and St. Francis de Sales, whom Pius IX proclaimed Doctors of the Church; the homage of the Christian world as it honored Pius IX on his priestly Jubilee; and the definitions of the dogmas of the Immaculate Conception and of papal infallibility.

As we exit the Pius IX Chapel, we turn to our left and walk through the impressive nineteenth-century sacristy to one of the loveliest parts of the basilica complex, the cloister. This island of tranquillity dates to Pope Clement III (1187-1191) and is one of the most ancient in Rome. It is, in fact, part of what remains of the fortified area we saw earlier, Lawrenceopolis. The very first monastery linked to this cloister dates from the eighth century. For the next eleven hundred years there was always a monastery, with different religious orders in charge, until the Capuchin friars were assigned to its care in 1857.

The two-story, rectangular cloister, with its dozens of pillars and arches of diverse sizes opening onto a lovely garden and mini-fountain, is bordered by four broad, covered passages. The walls of these passages are a veritable museum of stones, a lapidary's dream. There are hundreds and hundreds of pieces of stone and marble, large and small, embedded in the walls: pagan epigrams and tombstones, vestiges of catacombs, classical sarcophagi, fragments from the Constantinian basilica, and medieval stone cuttings, to name but a few. An entrance to the catacombs of St. Ciriaca can be found on one of the sides.

As we conclude our visit to St. Lawrence Outside-the-Walls, I have one piece of advice for visitors. Unless you are part of a large tour group that has prearranged a guided visit, it is best to go in the morning, as that is the only time of day that someone will be available to accompany you to the catacombs and to the Pius IX Chapel.

BASILICA OF THE HOLY CROSS IN JERUSALEM

As we have seen, the first Christian emperor, Constantine, played a preeminent role in the building of four of the five papal basilicas we have visited so far: St. Peter, St. John Lateran, St. Paul Outside-the-Walls, and St. Lawrence Outside-the-Walls. Our pilgrimage today takes us to the Basilica of the Holy Cross in Jerusalem, where not Constantine but his mother, the empress St. Helena, was the inspiration for the church we see today.

In fact, the story of St. Helena, her conversion to Christianity, her travels to the Holy Land and her recovery of relics linked to Christ's Passion and death, which she subsequently brought to Rome, is as interesting—and, in a way, as beautiful—as the church itself. St. Helena's faith, her devotion to the Cross and, of course, the relics themselves—part of the True Cross, a nail, thorns from the Crown of Thorns, and the wooden inscription affixed to the Cross bearing the words in three languages: "Jesus of Nazareth, King of the Jews"—these are all the very raison d'être for the basilica.

It must be recalled here that the Cross held great importance for Constantine the Great, who, as we saw earlier, had a vision on the vigil of the battle of Ponte Milvio, in which he saw a ray of light in the shape of a cross and heard the words "In this sign you shall conquer." Constantine and his mother were both converted to Christianity shortly after this vision and subsequent victory in battle.

As a sign of love for Christ and His Church, Constantine went to the Holy Land in 323, where he decided to build a mammoth basilica at Golgotha and at Christ's sepulcher. He intended to destroy the pagan temple that the emperor Hadrian (117-138), jealous and fearful of the followers of Christ, had built over the area where Christ was crucified and buried and the spot where relics associated with His death were buried. You will recall that, at the time of Christ's death, Jews were forbidden from burying condemned people in the communal cemetery, as this was considered to be a profanation. Items or instruments associated with the dead person had to be buried separately.

Constantine asked Bishop Macarius of Jerusalem to supervise the work. The architect was a priest from Constantinople named Eustacius. There were actually two churches: the Martyrion, built on the site of the Crucifixion, and the Anastasis, on the site of the sepulcher. The complex was consecrated on September 14, 335. Today, that date marks the feast of the Exaltation of the Cross, as that is allegedly the day on which St. Helena found the True Cross years earlier.

Helena, albeit in her eighties, had joined her son in Jerusalem at the time of the demolition of Hadrian's temple. Although she was an august personage in her own right as the mother of an emperor, Helena was known for her simplicity, humility, and good works. She called herself "the servant of the servants of Christ," and her motto was: "Prayer and good works." When she died, she was proclaimed a saint by the people, *vox populi*, as was the custom at the time.

It was Helena's love of the Cross that made her want to bring it from the oblivion of burial to the light of day, where Christians everywhere could pay it homage. After Hadrian's temple was razed, Helena spent hour after hour, digging with the workers in the dirt where they believed the relics of Christ's Passion to be. According to historians, Helena's first find was the *Elogium*, the wooden tablet that was placed above Christ's head on the Cross with the inscription in Greek, Hebrew, and Latin: "Jesus of Nazareth, King of the Jews."

Shortly afterward three crosses were discovered, the two on which the thieves were crucified and that on which Christ died. Which was Christ's? Bishop Macarius thought he had a solution. The three crosses were brought to the home of a saintly woman on her deathbed. They touched her with the first cross, and her agonies worsened. The same happened with the second cross. But when they touched her with the third, she was miraculously healed and arose from her deathbed.

The historian Rufinus preserved Bishop Macarius's prayer before this attempt to discover the True Cross: "Lord, you who gave salvation to mankind through the death on the Cross of your Only Begotten Son, and who now has inspired your servant [Helena] to seek the blessed wood where He hung for our salvation, show us which of these crosses served for divine glory and which served for the evildoers. Cause this woman, who is lying on her deathbed, to rise immediately upon touching the healing wood."

Helena bought to Rome not only large pieces of the True Cross but the Elogium, or Inscription, a nail used in the Crucifixion, two thorns (the Crown of Thorns today is in Notre Dame Cathedral in Paris: most of the thorns are missing as they were given as gifts to popes or to churches over the centuries), and soil from Calvary.

A private palace known as the *Sessorianum* had been given by Constantine to his mother as her residence. Shortly after her return from Jerusalem, and before her death, Helena decided to build a chapel there to house these relics of Christ's Passion. The ground of that chapel—the forerunner of the basilica we see today—was covered with the soil from Jerusalem; thus, the name Holy Cross in Jerusalem. Before its actual name, the basilica was also known as the Sessorian Basilica and the Helena Basilica.

Consecrated to the Holy Cross by Pope Sylvester I in the fourth century, the church was restored under Gregory II in 716 and again under Adrian I (772-795). It was altered in 1144 under Lucius II, taking the form of a three-aisled Roman basilica, and the bell tower was built. Further embellishments were added following the rediscovery of the Inscription on the Cross on February 1, 1492, during work being done on the roof and the ceiling. In earlier years it has been the custom to place relics in a high or inaccessible place to keep thieves from stealing the precious mementoes.

The basilica's current appearance dates to the pontificate of Benedict IV in the mid-eighteenth century. The only Pope buried

here is Benedict VII (974-983), who founded the adjacent monastery. In 1561 the monastery was entrusted to the Cistercians of
St. Saba. They still occupy the basilica and since 1910 have cared
for the parish attached to it.

The sheer size, majesty, and beauty of the other basilicas we
have seen can leave one somewhat disappointed upon entering
the Basilica of the Holy Cross in Jerusalem. The façade and the
interior are smaller than we are accustomed to seeing, and less
luxurious in decoration, but surprises await us.

The Baroque façade, commissioned by Pope Benedict XIV,
dates from 1743 and consists of four large columns forming three
portals, all of which is surmounted by bright windows. On the
balustrade we see statues of two angels holding the Cross, the
four Evangelists, St. Helena, and Emperor Constantine. As we
look up, our attention is also drawn to the eight-story bell tower,
completely built of bricks, with two bells from the seventeenth
century. A third was added in 1957. Granite columns from the
older basilica form part of the classical atrium.

The interior does not captivate the visitor as overwhelmingly
as did those of previously visited basilicas. Part of this is due to
its relatively small size. And part is due to the lack of light, giving
everything a more subdued appearance. The façade, transept, apse,
and Chapel of St. Helena all underwent extensive renovations for
the Holy Year 2000.

There is a central nave, flanked by two side aisles. Four of the
earlier granite columns remain. Our attention is drawn to both
the wooden ceiling, dominated by the coat of arms of Benedict
XIV, who commissioned it, and to the restored cosmatesque floor.

Standing in the apse area, we glance up at the ceiling, where
we note a painting of Christ set in a medallion and situated over
the main altar. The pillars surrounding the altar itself are from

the original basilica, but the canopy or baldachin dates from the eighteenth century. A casket below the altar contains the limbs of Sts. Caesariu and Anastasius. Rich frescoes cover the apse and depict scenes of Christ's Passion, stories of Helena's search for and discovery of the True Cross, Constantine's recognition of Christianity, and the Vision of the Cross in the heavens at the Last Judgment.

Moving to the far end of the right aisle, we come to the entrance to St. Helena's Chapel, an underground chapel and the oldest part of the basilica, which for a thousand years housed all of the relics linked to Christ's Passion. An inscription on the floor recounts that Helena transferred soil from Jerusalem, from Calvary, to this spot. In earlier years pilgrims tried to dig up the floor in order to secure a piece of soil, but the floor has since been reinforced to prevent this. Among the remarkable art works in the chapel are a statue of St. Helena (said to be a copy of a statue of Juno in the Vatican Museums) carrying the Cross, and the stunning mosaics on the vault that depict the finding of the Cross, the empress dividing it into parts, the procession with Bishop St. Macarius carrying the newly found Cross into Jerusalem, and the consecration of the chapel by Sylvester I.

Until 1935 women were allowed to visit this chapel only once a year, on March 20. In fact, the passageway separating the St. Helena Chapel from its neighboring St. Gregory Chapel is closed off by a huge iron gate. On the left side of the arched gateway a stone tablet was placed in the wall, reading: "Women cannot enter this holy chapel of Jerusalem, under pain of excommunication, except on one day a year, that is, on the day dedicated to it which falls on March 20." The most plausible explanation, according to some historians, was that this chapel was contiguous to the monastery and, to enter it, would have meant passing through the monastery, thus violating the cloistered rule. The prohibition was lifted by Pope Pius XI in order to avoid overcrowding, especially during pilgrimages and important liturgical moments. It also allowed greater numbers of the faithful to see the relics.

Returning to the basilica, to the left of the main altar, at the far end of the left aisle, there is a corridor that leads us down to the Chapel of St. Gregory, also known as the Chapel of the *Pietà*, so named for the marble *Pietà* on the high altar. Once visitors could reach this chapel directly from the Chapel of St. Helena, but this entrance has been closed.

Now we are ready to visit the Chapel of the Relics, the reason for our pilgrimage to the Basilica of the Holy Cross in Jerusalem.

On the far side of the left aisle is a door leading to what was once a sacristy but which, it was decided, in view of the 1925 Holy Year, had to be converted into a larger space to house the relics and welcome visitors. The relics had already been moved once in 1570 from St. Helena's Chapel, due to its extreme humidity and dampness, to a chapel behind the balcony and beyond the corridor to the right of the choir. Although the relics were now better protected, the new chapel afforded less access to the faithful. In fact, on certain great feast days, the relics were shown to the faithful from the balcony, as the chapel could not accommodate everyone.

Work on the current chapel began in 1930, well after the Holy Year, and ended in 1952, but it was only in late 1997 that all the relics were brought together in one room.

As we enter this door to the former sacristy, we find ourselves in a large, somber rectangular room—almost reminiscent of a mausoleum—that the architect intended to be the Hill of Calvary. In fact, it is an uphill walk to the actual chapel—beyond fourteen bronze Stations of the Cross set in niches and nine large stone slabs with Latin inscriptions about the meaning of the Cross.

Before proceeding up this passage, however, we stop before the 1.78-meter beam from the cross of the Good Thief, St. Dismas, encased in glass and behind a metal latticework just opposite the entrance.

On our own, small pilgrimage to Calvary, we reach the top of this passage and enter a small anteroom. On our right we see a metal grill, also called a rood screen or choir screen, whose doorway leads us directly to the Chapel of the Relics. The floor and walls of the relic room are in lush marble. Particularly suggestive on the walls of both the vestibule and the chapel are the "niches" created of cut marble that have at their center tall, slender candles of black marble. The workmanship is so extraordinary that the walls seem indeed to have niches with candelabras, rather than flat surfaces.

There are also two lovely stained-glass windows near the top of the left wall. A doorway on the right wall brings you to a small, elongated room with a replica of the Shroud of Turin on one wall.

The relics themselves are in magnificent reliquaries on three shelves of a shatterproof glass enclosure on the far wall of the chapel.

As you enter the Chapel of Relics, three pews beckon you to prayer. The pews are in front of a baldacchino that once covered an altar. The altar is no longer there so, as you pray, you are looking beyond the canopy to the far wall and the six reliquaries.

On the top shelf, there are three relics: On the left is the index finger of St. Thomas, the doubting Thomas who wished to put his finger into Christ's wounds before he would believe the Lord had risen. Not all historians agree as to its provenance, but many, in their writings, included the finger among those relics brought to Rome by St. Helena. A small reliquary in the center of this shelf contains miniscule stone fragments from the column where Christ was scourged, from the Cave of the Nativity and from the Holy Sepulcher. On the right side of this shelf is the reliquary with two thorns from the Crown of Thorns worn by Jesus.

Earlier I mentioned that the Crown of Thorns is actually in the Cathedral of Notre Dame de Paris. It is described as "a circle of canes bundled together and held by gold threads. The thorns were attached to this braided circle, which measures 21 centimetres in diameter. The thorns were divided up over the centuries by the Byzantine emperors and the Kings of France. There are seventy, all of the same type, which have been confirmed as the original thorns."

On the middle shelf is a single reliquary—a breathtakingly beautiful relic holder of gold, silver, and lapis lazuli made by Giuseppe Valadier in 1803—that contains three pieces of the True Cross, all that remained after St. Helena donated pieces to the Pope and to other churches. They are placed in the lateral arms and the lower portion of the cross-shaped reliquary that was donated by Spanish Duchess Villahermosa in 1803.

The bottom shelf has two reliquaries: On the left we see one of the nails that pierced Jesus' flesh, and on the right, the Titulus placed above His head on the Cross.

The nail is one of three that Helena brought back from the Holy Land. The other two were given to her son, Emperor Constantine, but both have been lost over time. The nail measures 12.5 centimeters in length.

The glass and gold reliquary that is on the right side of this shelf holds the Titulus, at least what remains of the Inscription on the Cross in three languages, the same inscription found in 1492 behind a seal with the words *Titulus Crucis*. This seal is now in the wall of the anteroom to the chapel, on our right as we enter. This relic was found accidentally during restoration work on the basilica that had been commissioned by Spanish titular cardinal Pietro Gonzales de Mendoza, in the thirteenth century. Experts all say the inscription is compatible with the references in the Bible that mention the letters INRI and the words "Jesus of Nazareth, King of the Jews."

As I sat in the silence of this chapel and tried to meditate on these relics, I had two thoughts. The first was how sadly limited we mortals are in our ability truly to contemplate, to comprehend the meaning of these relics, these pieces of wood and metal that seem like mere objects but are, in reality, intrinsically linked to our salvation. Perhaps we expect to be struck with ecstasy, with awesome understanding—and we are disappointed.

My second thought was: How can I write about something for which there are no words?

Those are my thoughts. My hope for you is that you do not leave Rome without visiting the Basilica of the Holy Cross in Jerusalem. It is a *very* special pilgrimage, a trip to the very meaning of our lives.

BASILICA OF ST. SEBASTIAN

The last of the seven major basilicas of Rome to be visited on our pilgrimage is the church that is built above the catacombs of the same name and is dedicated to the third-century saint who was twice martyred.

The first mention of St. Sebastian dates back to a fourth-century entry in the Roman Church Calendar that refers to the saint's January 20 feast day. St. Ambrose, bishop of Milan at the end of that same century, in a letter to the Milanese faithful marking that day, wrote: "The example of St. Sebastian, whose feast is today, should help us: he was a native of Milan."

Little is known of the saint, although a tale called "The Passion of St. Sebastian," dating to the time of Pope Sixtus III (432-440). recounts that he was a member of the elite First Praetorian Cohort of the Emperor Maximianus (co-emperor with Diocletian), who denounced him for his preaching of the gospel and condemned him to be shot to death by archers. Sebastian was found still alive by Irene, the widow of St. Castulus, who nursed him back to health. Once recovered, he returned to the emperor, who ordered him to be taken to the Palatine Circus and beaten to death. The tale continues: Sebastian appeared in a dream to a lady named Lucina, telling her that his body could be found in the sewers, where it was thrown after his beating, and asking her to bring it to the catacombs and bury it near the remains of the Apostles Peter and Paul.

St. Sebastian today, however, is always depicted with arrows piercing his body. He is the patron of athletes and archers.

St. Sebastian's body remained in his tomb in the catacombs until 826, when Pope Eugene II had it removed to the Vatican, to a special altar in the Oratory of St. Gregory the Great. The head and other relics were later given to the Church of the Quattro Coronati (the Four Crowned Saints). Pope Honorius III (1216-1227), answering petitions by the faithful as well as by the Cistercian monks officiating at the basilica, ordered the relics to be returned to the catacombs and deposited in an ancient cosmatesque altar in the crypt, an altar that he personally reconsecrated. When Cardinal Scipione Borghese restored the church in the seventeenth century, he transferred this altar to the basilica itself, placing it against the left wall. We will see this shortly.

BASILICA OF ST. PETER

I once heard someone say that if architecture is frozen music, St. Peter's Basilica is a symphony. As we visit the largest of the seven pilgrim churches, we see the grandeur, the glory, and the sheer immensity of the church built over the tomb of the first Pope, St. Peter. This papal basilica also houses three relics of the Passion of Our Lord: the spear that pierced Christ's side, Veronica's veil, and pieces of wood from the True Cross. They are in a relic room above the statue of St. Helena, in a niche in one of the four piers that support the dome.

Basilica of St. John Lateran

St. John Lateran is the cathedral church of the Bishop of Rome, the Pope. In this photo we see the principal façade with the colossal travertine statues. The original basilica was built by Emperor Constantine, who had converted to Christianity and granted Christians religious freedom in the Edict of Milan in 313. He wanted this church to be the greatest, the mother, of all churches, and we see a plaque to this effect on the façade: "The Most Holy Church of the Lateran, Mother of all the churches of Rome and of the world." Across the street from the basilica is the *Scala Santa*, or Holy Staircase, said to be the twenty-eight steps on which Jesus walked to Pilate's house in Jerusalem.

In this photo, we see St. John Lateran's so-called second façade, the north façade, which is actually a double portico built by Domenico Fontana and frescoed by artists of the sixteenth century. Here we find the Loggia of Blessings from which popes used to bless the populace. Atop the porticoes are two twelfth-century bell towers, and in the square in front of this entrance is one of twelve remaining Egyptian obelisks in Rome. Many offices of the Vicariate of Rome are located in the floors above this entrance.

BASILICA OF ST. PAUL
OUTSIDE-THE-WALLS

St. Paul Outside-the-Walls, also built by the first Christian emperor, Constantine, is the second-largest church in Rome and stands on the burial place of the Apostle Paul. What has been called the "trademark feature" of this basilica is the series of mosaic portraits of all the popes from St. Peter to Pope Francis that are located above the columns of the right nave. Legend says that when the last portrait is done, the world will end. How many are left? You will have to read this chapter!

BASILICA OF ST. MARY MAJOR

St. Mary Major, one of the four papal basilicas of Rome, is also known as Our Lady of the Snows. On the night of August 5, 358, Our Lady appeared in a dream to a Roman patrician couple and to Pope Liberius and requested that a church be built in her honor where snow would fall that night. The three kept their promise to Our Lady, and the feast of Our Lady of the Snows is commemorated every year on August 5. Beneath the main altar of this basilica is a small chapel that houses relics of the manger crib in which the Christ Child was laid in Bethlehem.

BASILICA OF ST. LAWRENCE
OUTSIDE-THE-WALLS

St. Lawrence Outside-the-Walls, also known as St. Lawrence at Verano, covers centuries of history because we have parts of the original fourth-century Constantinian basilica, part of the sixth-century basilica built by Pope Pelagius, and the thirteenth-century addition ordered by Pope Honorius III. St. Lawrence was a deacon of the Church who was burned alive in 258. A cult had arisen around him, and Emperor Constantine was one of Lawrence's devotees. Sts. Lawrence, Stephen, and Justin are buried in the *confessio*.

BASILICA OF THE HOLY CROSS IN JERUSALEM

It was not the Christian emperor Constantine who was responsible for building the basilica of the Holy Cross in Jerusalem, but rather his mother, Empress Helena, who was the inspiration for the church we see today. From the Holy Land, St. Helena brought to Rome relics of the Passion of Christ: pieces of the True Cross, a nail, thorns from the crown of thorns, and the wood inscription on the Cross that said in three languages "Jesus of Nazareth, King of the Jews." There is also the finger of St. Thomas, doubting Thomas, who said he would believe that Christ has risen only if he could put his finger into Christ's wounds.

BASILICA OF ST. SEBASTIAN

St. Sebastian was a third-century martyr condemned to die during the persecution of Christians by co-emperors Maximianus and Diocletian. He was to be shot to death with arrows, but he survived, only to be clubbed to death later. Sebastian, however, is typically pictured as tied to a tree, with arrows piercing his body. His tomb is in a chapel on the left side of the basilica that was built above the catacombs of the same name. This basilica is also designated as *memoria Apostolorum* because there was a period when the faithful used to gather here to venerate the remains of Sts. Peter and Paul. Sebastian is the patron saint of athletes and archers.

The Seven Pilgrimage Basilicas

The Basilica of St. Sebastian and the catacombs beneath it are inseparable in their history, which comprises four distinct periods. The first, mainly pagan, dates from the first to the middle of the third century. The second, both pagan and Christian, dates from about 250 to 330. The third period, Christian, lasts from the building of the Church in the first half of the fourth century to the Middle Ages. The final period dates from the end of the sixteenth century to the present.

The first basilica, much larger than the present one, was originally called the Basilica of the Apostles. It had a nave and two aisles and a colonnaded ambulatory, later narrowed down to the present single nave. We will see in the chapter dedicated to the catacombs that very often basilicas were built underground, in the catacombs themselves, in commemoration of a particular saint or saints. Later, to accommodate increased numbers of pilgrims coming to visit the tombs or relics of these saints, larger basilicas were built above ground, over the saints' tombs.

St. Sebastian's Basilica was termed—and still is today—in memoriam Apostolorum, "in the memory of the Apostles," because, for a period, the faithful had gathered in these catacombs to venerate the remains of the two Apostles. There are various theories as to why pilgrims came here: some scholars believe that the Apostles lived here for a time; others say that their remains were brought here to make it possible to commemorate the two great Apostles jointly; yet others believe their relics were brought to these catacombs for safekeeping. Remember, we are not yet in the time of Emperor Constantine, the first Christian emperor and the first to allow Christians to profess their faith openly and freely. In any case, as we shall shortly see, remarkable evidence exists that the relics of Peter and Paul were indeed brought here and jointly venerated around the year 250.

Within this underground cemetery on the Via Appia Antica, a small portico had been raised, overlooking a courtyard at a lower level, from which steps descended, leading to a well. On the rear wall of the portico, there was a mason bench. This whole structure, found in other catacombs as well, was called the *triclia*, that is, a place near a sepulcher where funerary banquets, called *refrigerium* (refreshments), took place, and where the faithful gathered to commemorate the deceased.

In this particular case, what made it so special was that, above the bench, on the wall of the portico—still visible today behind a protective Plexiglas wall—were over six hundred graffiti inscribed to the memory of the Apostles Peter and Paul. Repeated mention was made of *refrigeria* in their memory. Of these graffiti, not a single mention is made of another person—just the two Apostles.

The *Liber Pontificalis*, or *Book of the Popes*, which contained biographies of early pontiffs, recounts that Pope Damasus (366-384), who had a passion for writing verses to memorialize saints and martyrs, had the following inscribed on a slab adorning the site where the bodies of the Apostles rested: "Here you should know that the saints once dwelt, you who are seeking the names of both Peter and Paul. The Orient sent us these Apostles, we admit it willingly, but through their martyrdom, following Christ above in the celestial spheres and in the Kingdom of the righteous, Rome was enabled to claim them as her citizens: This is, O new stars, what Damasus wanted to say in your praise."

The old basilica, about 2,000 square meters in size, was erected above this *memoriam Apostolorum* and covered the entire area now occupied by the museum, the choir, the two sacristies, and the Albani Chapel. Built around 340, during the reign of Pope Julius, it followed a typical Constantinian basilica form of a nave (which was covered by a timber roof) and two aisles circling the apse to join together.

It is generally believed that this basilica was not dedicated to St. Sebastian until the Middle Ages, although there are records indicating that Pope St. Gregory the Great (590-604) delivered a homily here on the feast of St. Sebastian, thus suggesting to some that the church was already dedicated to this saint. A legend linked to this Pope relates that while he was celebrating Mass here, an angel appeared to him, saying: "In this place we find the truth of the promise and redemption of sinners, the splendor, the eternal light and the endless bliss which the martyr of Christ Sebastian merited." This inscription today is over the door of the old sacristy.

Modifications and changes to the façade and the inside of the basilica were made over the centuries, and what we see today dates mostly from the early seventeenth century.

A small walled courtyard, just off the Via Appia Antica, welcomes us to the basilica, whose two-tiered façade was commissioned by Cardinal Scipione Borghese and designed by Flaminio Ponzio. The upper tier has three large windows and the Borghese coat of arms. The lower tier, leading to the atrium and the basilica entrance, consists of three arcades resting on six Ionic columns, four in red granite and two in gray Egyptian granite. An inscription marks this as the work of Cardinal Borghese and dates it to 1612.

The central door leads to the church, whereas the door to our right leads to the ticket office and entrance to the catacombs, a spacious waiting area whose walls are decorated by fragments of stones and marble that were once part of tombs or mausoleums in the catacombs. The catacombs themselves are, on the average, 17 meters below the actual basilica.

Entering the basilica, we are struck by its luminosity, something notably missing from the other churches we have visited.

As it has only a single nave, we are able to observe the church's features — the ceiling, floor, and side chapels — unfettered by columns or other distractions.

First off, we note the elaborate wood coffered ceiling, at whose center is the figure of St. Sebastian. Cardinal Borghese's coat of arms also appears. The pavement, simple and smooth, unlike the rich cosmatesque art of geometrical shapes to which we have become accustomed, was recently redone in Veronese marble.

On our left, near the entrance, is the only inscription by Pope Damasus to have survived to the present, unbroken and intact. Dedicated to St. Eutychius, it was first placed in the crypt of St. Sebastian but was transferred to the basilica in the sixteenth century. It describes in minute detail the sufferings of this saint who was martyred with Sebastian and Quirinus and buried in the catacombs beneath the basilica. Pope Damasus did much to support the veneration of Christian martyrs, writing often about individual saints, as we see in this inscription.

On this same wall is the ornate marble Chapel and Altar of St. Sebastian. We saw that Cardinal Borghese, in 1612, had brought St. Sebastian's altar from the catacombs to the basilica. Around 1672 Cardinal Francesco Barberini commissioned the chapel we see today, small yet suggestive, and lovely with its polychrome marble.

Behind a huge metal grate is the altar table where an urn containing the remains of the saint had been placed. Beneath the altar is a marble statue of St. Sebastian, commissioned by Cardinal Barberini, as he imagined the saint to be at his martyrdom, that is, with arrows piercing his body, which is partially wrapped in a shroud.

Just across the way is the Altar of the Relics, housed in a chapel whose decoration was ordered by Maximilian, Duke of Bavaria, in 1625. Above the altar, encased in glass are reliquaries containing one of the arrows that pierced St. Sebastian (left) and the column to which he was tied when the archers shot him (right). In the center is the so-called *Quo Vadis* slab with the imprints of Jesus' feet when he appeared to St. Peter on the Old Appian Way. According to legend, St. Peter was fleeing Rome and the persecutions of the emperor Nero. He met the Lord on his way out of the city and asked Him, *"Quo vadis, Domine?"* (Where are you going, Lord?). When the Lord replied that he was going to Rome to be crucified a second time, St. Peter, understanding his own destiny, returned to Rome to suffer martyrdom along with his fellow Christians. In fact, there is a church named Quo Vadis, near the basilica of St. Sebastian, built on the site where this encounter allegedly took place.

Proceeding up the right side of the church, to the right of the high altar, we come to the only other chapel, the Albani Chapel, the largest and most richly decorated of the three in the basilica. It was dedicated to St. Fabian, who was co-patron of this church with St. Sebastian and whose remains are believed to rest in a sarcophagus under the floor in the center of the chapel.

Pope Clement XI (1706-1712), a member of the Albani family, had this chapel erected as a sepulchral chapel for the members of his family. The quadrangular chapel, with apse and dome, was designed by Carlo Fontana. Its beauty comes from its magnificent bronze and wrought-iron railings, statues, stuccoes, and precious marbles. A statue of St. Fabian, represented as a seventeenth-century Pope, dominates the altar. This chapel used to have its own sacristy. That was transformed into a museum, and in 1916 it became the basilica's main sacristy. A staircase descends from the sacristy to a columbarium decorated with second-century stuccoes. The richly decorated sarcophagus of Orazio Albani, Clement

XI's brother, lies below the chapel and requires special permission to visit.

Now we return to the apse and the main altar, reconstructed by Cardinal Barberini with material from the catacombs and the previous altar. The altar is covered by a canopy resting on four columns of green marble. The apse ceiling was restored by Pope Gregory XVI (1831-1846).

Doors on the left wall lead to the epigraphic museum and to the basilica's ancient left nave, where there is a plastic model reconstruction of the first basilica and the fourth-century mausoleums built around it. Nearby is a staircase from which visitors to the catacombs exit. Between the two doors, inside the basilica, is an altar dedicated to St. Francis.

After visiting the basilica, you will want to visit the catacombs — unless you did this when you first arrived, in order to have a better appreciation of the entire history of the church.

We will take an in-depth look at the catacombs in the chapter dedicated to them, but it is obligatory here to list the highlights of the catacomb of St. Sebastian. The premiere site is, without any doubt, the triclia area with its wall of graffiti dedicated to the Apostles Peter and Paul. The second most important site is the crypt dedicated to the saint, featuring a bust of Sebastian attributed to Bernini.

It might be worth mentioning (if you haven't already guessed!) that visitors are not allowed to roam the catacombs freely and unescorted; only guided tours are allowed. No photos or videos are allowed. Most guides will take you to the places I am about to mention, although there are some tours of abbreviated length that do not include all of them. The triclia graffiti wall of Sts. Peter and Paul and the tomb of St. Sebastian are, however, always included.

The other noteworthy spots of the Sebastian catacomb are the cubicle of St. Philip Neri; the *arcosolium* in gallery 3, featuring traces of a painting of the Crib; the cubicle of Jonah, discovered in 1950, with its four frescoes depicting the biblical episode of Jonah and the whale; and the astonishing Roman villa built around a large, square courtyard, with a reception room paved in black-and-white marble, and whose walls are decorated with architectural designs and pictures.

There is a kind of fork in the road in gallery 9: one path will take you to the Roman villa, and a second will take you to the Piazzuola, or little square, nine meters under the floor of the basilica, to the south of its foundations.

Here we see the façades of what look like three small homes, but which are stately mausoleums. Entirely hewn into the rock and rising to a great height, the façades are of masonry and brickwork and date to the first half of the second century. The entryways are of travertine. Above the doors are rectangular spaces that were intended for the *tituli*, the marble plates on which were inscribed the names of the families whose members are entombed. Each entrance is crowned by a tympanum, a triangular recessed space. Low walls rising above the tympanum formed a sort of terrace area called a *solaria*, which served as a meeting place at the time of a burial when small banquets, the *refrigeria*, took place.

The mausoleum to our right is called the Mausoleum of Marcus Clodius Hermes, given the inscriptions on it. In fact, its titulus tells us that M. Clodius Hermes lived to be seventy-five years of age! The next one is called the Mausoleum of the Innocentiores: the lintel over the door bears a tablet with an inscription bearing the name of the praetorian L. Hostilius Castor, a native of Potenza. One of the chambers of the lower story of this mausoleum has graffiti consisting of the Greek word for fish. For early Christians the acronym of this Greek word, with a *T* inserted for the Cross, represented "Jesus Christ, Son of God, Savior." The last mausoleum, the one to our far left, standing against the basilica's foundations, has been given the name Mausoleum of the Ax, because of the two-bladed ax depicted in a stucco relief in the tympanum.

Each mausoleum has two stories, the lower one accessible by a staircase. The *loculi*, the rectangular openings carved into the walls for the bodies of the deceased (we shall study this further in the chapter on the catacombs), were not usually sealed with a marble slab, as one would see in simpler graves in the catacombs, but rather were sealed with bricks.

The most astonishing element of these mausoleums is their decorations, the vibrant ornamental frescoes, considered to be Christian, the elaborate mosaic floors, the lunettes, stuccoes, and bas-reliefs. It staggers the imagination to think that almost eighteen centuries have passed!

We've only scratched the surface of what the basilica and catacombs of St. Sebastian have to offer, but I hope it has whetted your appetite for a more prolonged visit.

Chapter VI

THE CATACOMBS

The Roman catacombs are among the most venerated places of Christianity and a premier attraction for both pilgrims and tourists. Not only do they represent positively remarkable engineering feats, but they are, as well, rich repositories of material that, notwithstanding centuries of sacking, have provided us with valuable insights into Christian life, death, worship, and art of the first centuries.

Literally hundreds of kilometers of these underground cemeteries were built on the perimeter of Imperial Rome, along the great consular roads of Ostiense, the Appia Antica or Old Appian Way, Via Tiburtina, Via Salaria, and Via Nomentana, because it was forbidden by Roman law to bury the dead within city limits. The city's limits, defined by an imaginary line known as the *pomerium*, were expanded over time and, as a result, catacombs were also built further and further out. More than forty catacombs have been counted within a few miles of the Aurelian Walls, although only a handful are open today to visitors.

To digress for a moment, the consular roads had their own interesting history. The Via Ostiense (which we saw when we went to

A HOLY YEAR IN ROME

St. Paul Outside-the-Walls) led to the seaport of Ostia, where the Romans kept their navy. The Appia Antica—still paved in part today with the enormous stones of Imperial Roman times—extended all the way to the Adriatic seaport of Brindisi, where the Roman navy was also stationed for its travels to the Eastern Empire and where today one can see traces of the Appia Antica and several ancient Roman pillars. The road was named for the censor Appius Claudius, who began building it in 312. The Via Salaria, leading north out of Rome, was the site of salt quarries (*sale* means "salt"), and at one time, when funds were low, Roman soldiers were paid in salt, a highly prized commodity.

What archaeologists discovered over time in excavating the catacomb areas was just how well ordered and efficient the Christian communities of the first centuries were. The community was, in fact, organized into districts called *tituli*, equivalent to modern-day parishes. These in turn were organized into ecclesiastical regions, each of which was assigned a burial area outside the city. Evidence of this organization has been found in the catacombs, and also in the Liberian Catalogue of 354, which documented in a lively fashion the lives of the third-century popes.

In some instances, the land used for above-ground cemeteries, as well as the catacombs, belonged to wealthy families who donated it to the Christian community. Often a larger portion of the cemetery or catacombs was designated for the donor family, and traces of their burial plots can be seen in the more elaborate tombs and even mini-chapels. Indeed, some of the catacombs have names that were difficult to trace, and it was deduced that the name was that of the wealthy donor. Most of the more-well-known catacombs, however, bear the names of martyrs.

All underground catacombs were once linked to cemeteries above ground that contained elaborate sarcophagi. Few vestiges of these surface cemeteries remain today, whereas, as we said earlier, there are still hundreds of kilometers of catacombs.

While it was thought for a time that the catacombs were burial places only for Christian martyrs, exploration and excavations showed that these were burial areas for pagans, Jews, and Christians, in particular the poor. Whereas wealthy or noble citizens could have a mausoleum or burial plot above ground, Jews and Christians for the most part could not afford such plots. Nor did they allow cremation, as Romans did. Thus, the only place to go was below ground.

Originally each catacomb was only a very small nucleus of burial chambers. As Christianity spread, and as eventually there were more Christians to bury, the catacombs grew in height, depth, length, and complexity. By the fourth century most catacombs had developed into an amazing labyrinth of chambers, passageways, altars, and mini-basilicas—a veritable necropolis. The Christian gravediggers, in fact, had acquired truly marvelous technical expertise.

Galleries were usually dug to a width of 1 meter, to allow people to pass, and a height of 2 or 3 meters, and wells, or skylights, were created for light and ventilation. Rectangular cavities, the exact size of the person to be buried, were dug into the walls. The deceased was laid in the cavity, or *loculus*, and covered with a shroud, usually coated with lime as an easy form of embalming. This was then closed with a lime-coated slab. Occasionally, two bodies were buried in the same loculus. The name of the deceased was then engraved or painted on the slab, sometimes accompanied by his age, his date of death, and the name of the person who entombed him.

Over time, Christian elements were added to some of the tombs, either words or symbols: a dove for peace; a cross; an anchor, signaling a safe arrival. Later, eulogies or descriptions of the person's life or Christian attributes were also added.

The burial sites of wealthier people attested to their state of life and were more elaborate. This richer form of burial was known as the *arcosolium*, and consisted of a more decorative slab, above which was constructed an arch, often decorated with frescoes. The arcosolium was frequently used in the *cubicula*, small rooms that opened out from the passageways, a type of family mausoleum. The bigger the cubicula, the greater the decoration: arches, vaulted ceilings, cornicework, pillars, and frescoes. Sarcophagi can be found, but only rarely.

The artwork decorating the catacombs is quite refined for the first centuries. Hundreds of frescoes and mosaics—some still very rich in color—depict biblical scenes and parables, express belief in the Resurrection of Christ and eternal salvation, and teach about the sacraments, in particular Baptism and the Eucharist. The deceased are always pictured in an attitude of prayer, and the scenes surrounding them exude serenity and joy.

The tombs of the early saints and martyrs, which are, of course, the hallmark of the catacombs, are open to the public today, and they are what led to the great development of the catacombs in the early centuries. Devotion to the martyrs led many Christians to make pilgrimages to their burial places, and this is why we are here today. In fact, those catacombs dedicated to martyrs were—and are—among the most visited and well preserved.

Pope Damasus (366-384), a great admirer of the martyrs, sought out their tombs and restored and embellished them, ordering many of them to be inscribed, in elegant calligraphy, with verses he himself composed.

Over time, to make room for the ever-increasing number of pilgrims who wished to pray at the tombs of the martyrs, areas were

The Catacombs

enlarged, and small chapels or even basilicas were built. Larger liturgical gatherings took place, however, in the churches built above ground, over the tombs. We saw, for example, how Pope Honorius built the basilica over the tomb of St. Lawrence and over the catacombs of St. Ciriaca. For several centuries, until the end of the eighth century, when pilgrimages began to decline, specific itineraries were even mapped out for the faithful who wished to visit the catacombs and the tombs of the martyrs.

In time, due to sacking by the Vandals and Lombards, the suburban or peripheral areas of Rome were abandoned—and this included some of the catacombs. To safeguard the relics of saints and martyrs that were in the catacombs, many were brought to Rome and placed in churches. Catacombs fell into general disuse, and for centuries the precise location of some of them was not even known. Only a few continued to be visited during the Middle Ages.

A serendipitous discovery in 1578 of a nucleus of subterranean galleries with magnificent paintings on the Via Salaria led to renewed enthusiasm for the catacombs among historians, scholars, and archaeologists. One scholar, Antonio Bosio, even earned the name "Columbus of underground Rome" for his discoveries and subsequent erudite studies. While this led to great works, some less-well-intentioned archaeologists despoiled several of the catacombs, resulting in what we see today in some areas: damaged sarcophagi, broken stone funeral slabs, and the like.

Fortunately for us, Pope Pius IX set up the Pontifical Commission for Sacred Archeology in the last century, and the work of destruction came to an end. Today, thanks to the February 11, 1929, Lateran Pacts between Italy and the Holy See, the catacombs, by virtue of article 33, are entrusted to the Holy See, which sees to their exploration, care, and preservation.

A HOLY YEAR IN ROME

Of the seven catacombs open today to the public, the three most visited are St. Calixtus (Via Appia Antica 102), St. Sebastian (Via Appia Antica 134, where there is also the basilica of the same name), and Domitilla (Via delle Sette Chiese 282). The other catacombs that are open are Priscilla (Via Salaria Nuova), St. Lawrence Outside-the-Walls (Via Tiburtina), St. Agnes (Via Nomentana), and San Pancrazio (Via Vitellia).

St. Calixtus is the oldest of all the ancient cemeteries. All the popes of the third century (with the exception, oddly enough, of Calixtus himself), as well as three bishops—Optatus, Numidianus, and Urban—are buried here. It is believed that because of disturbances surrounding his martyrdom, Pope St. Calixtus is buried on the Via Aurelia in Calepodio. Inscriptions on the various tombs identify them as those of martyrs or bishops (*episcopus*). One of the most visited crypts here is that of St. Cecilia. In the niche, illuminated by a large skylight, is a copy of the famous statue by Maderno, depicting Cecilia at the moment of her death. The original is in the Basilica of Santa Cecilia in Rome's Trastevere neighborhood.

Behind the crypts of the popes and St. Cecilia is the vast primitive area of the catacombs, with its series of long, seemingly endless intertwining galleries, some as high as five stories, staircases, and six frescoed cubicula, known as the "cubicula of the Sacraments," where we see numerous references to the sacraments of Baptism and the Eucharist. Other martyrs buried here include Tarcisius, Calogerus, and Parthenius.

The catacombs of Domitilla contain a number of very large tombs and are, in extension, larger than St. Calixtus. They take their name from the martyr Domitilla, a relative of the emperor Domitian and daughter of the second consul Flavius Clemens. She died during the persecutions at the end of the first century.

The Catacombs

In addition to the endless labyrinth of galleries, the most outstanding feature of these catacombs is the large-aisled basilica built deep below the surface. The church is dedicated to Sts. Nereus and Achilleus, two soldier-martyrs who were later honored by Pope Damasus with one of his numerous inscriptions. The surrounding galleries were demolished to make room for the basilica, built between 390 and 395, whose altar was placed over their tomb.

The St. Sebastian catacombs were referred to in ancient documents as the Memorial of the Apostles, as it was on this spot that the Apostles Peter and Paul were first jointly venerated. Their remains had been transferred here from their tombs on the Via Ostiense (St. Paul) and on Vatican Hill (St. Peter) at a time when they were thought to be in considerable danger of profanation. It must be remembered that many relics were considered in danger for several reasons: either people simply wanted for themselves some reminder or remnant of the saint or martyr they venerated or, as was the case with civil authorities, especially those who were against the new Christian Faith, it was felt that by destroying a relic, they would destroy the faith of the followers.

Some historians believe there was no element of danger involved for the relics of the Apostles, but rather that they were brought here simply because it would be easier to venerate the two great Apostles together on their feast day in a single location. The oldest calendar of the Roman Church, in fact, gives June 29 as the joint feast of Sts. Peter and Paul, adding that this commemoration began in the year 258. Their relics have since been returned to the basilicas bearing their name, and June 29 is still their feast day. In their honor a great basilica was built here in the Constantinian period.

The devotion to St. Sebastian, for whom the catacombs are named, developed much later. The tomb where the saint's body had been placed during the persecutions by Emperor Diocletian was enlarged and embellished in the fifth century. Two centuries later, Sebastian's popularity grew among Romans when, during the plague of 680, many of them prayed for his intercession and were spared. In fact, Romans dedicated an altar to him in the church of St. Peter in Chains, near the Coliseum. Today the saint's remains are in the chapel dedicated to him in the Basilica of St. Sebastian (the first chapel on our left), and relics associated with his death are in the chapel on the opposite wall.

For a more in-depth look at these particular catacombs, you might want to go back to the story on the Basilica of St. Sebastian.

The catacombs of Priscilla are in the northern part of Rome, on the Via Salaria, the one named for the salt quarries. These are some of the most ancient and extensive of all the catacombs, and the name comes from the owner of the land, a member of the nobility as we see from the word *clarissima* on an epitaph. Numerous martyrs were buried here including Felix, Philip, Crescentius, Prisca, and Praxedes, to name but a few. Seven Popes were also buried here: Marcellinus (296-308), Marcellus (308-309), Sylvester I (314-335; one of the eleven longest pontificates in history), Liberius (352-366, known for building the Basilica of St. Mary Major, also known as the Liberian Basilica), Siricius (384-399), Celestine (422-432), and Vigilius (537-555).

The upper level of underground corridors is the most ancient of the network of corridors and contains paintings and stuccoes of the earliest Christian art, with scenes from the Old and New Testaments.

Noteworthy among the many frescoes is that of the *Breaking of the Bread*, with its references to the miracle of the loaves and fishes and to the Eucharistic banquet, and two paintings of the Virgin Mary, dating from the first half of the second century, considered the most ancient in existence. In one Mary is depicted with the Child Jesus in her arms and a prophet at her side. In the second, she is seated with an angel in front of her, a clear reference to the Annunciation.

Chapter VII

VATICAN CITY STATE

❖

Vatican City State was created as a result of the Lateran Pacts stipulated between the Holy See and the Kingdom of Italy on February 11, 1929, and ratified on June 7 of the same year. It is universally recognized as a legal entity and sovereign body of public international law distinct from the Holy See. UNESCO has declared the whole of the territory of Vatican City part of the world's cultural heritage.

All the territory of Vatican City State is under the protection of the Hague Convention of May 1954, regarding the care of cultural goods in case of armed conflict. The state is thus recognized, even in international conventions, as a moral, artistic, and cultural patrimony worthy of being respected and protected.

The government is an elective monarchy for life. The head of state is the Supreme Pontiff, who has full legislative, executive, and judicial powers. During the period of a vacant see — *sede vacante* — these powers are assumed by the Sacred College of Cardinals.

Vatican City State has its own currency and issues its own postage stamps, and both are very much in demand by collectors and everyday tourists to the Vatican. The letters on the license plate of Vatican automobiles are SCV (*Stato della Città del Vaticano*). Italians like to say that SCV stands for "*se Cristo vedesse*" — "if only Christ could see"!

Located on what many call the "eighth hill" of Rome, on the left bank of the Tiber River, Vatican City — the smallest state in the world — measures 108.7 acres, about the size of an average golf course, I have been told. It is bordered by the Leonine Walls and, just off St. Peter's Square, by the circular travertine strip in the pavement that joins the two arms of the Bernini colonnades.

This lovely, tranquil ministate, set in the midst of the hustle and bustle of Rome, is home to several hundred citizens, boasts splendid, centuries-old buildings, chapels, and churches, a pre-seminary, mosaic factory, fire department, and the famed Vatican Library, Secret Archives, and Vatican Museums. There is also a second-century necropolis, the *scavi*, under St. Peter's where the first Pope and the basilica's namesake is buried. It has stores, a pharmacy, gas stations, a printing office, and a medical center. It even has its own cemetery. There are also acres and acres of breathtaking gardens, some formal, some wild, all lush — dotted with stone benches, statuary, and unique fountains whose water comes from Lake Bracciano, 40 kilometers outside of Rome.

There are five entrances to Vatican City, all secured by Swiss Guards or members of the Vatican's police force or gendarmerie. The first is the Arch of the Bells (Arco delle Campane), a tunnel-like entrance to the left of St. Peter's Basilica. Then we have the Bronze Door (Portone di Bronzo), which is considered the official entrance to the Apostolic Palace and is situated at the juncture of the palace and the right-hand Bernini colonnade. Third is the St. Anne, or Sant'Anna entrance, which takes its name from the parish church located just inside Vatican City as you enter from Via di

Porta Angelica. The fourth entrance is the Petrine or Sant'Uffizio gate, by which one enters the Paul VI Hall, just outside the left-hand colonnade of St. Peter's Square. The fifth entrance—the least well known by the general public—is the Perugino on the south wall of the Vatican.

Vatican City State's four hundred–plus inhabitants include people of many nationalities, although most are Italian. Several hundred have Vatican citizenship, including those prelates who are heads of offices in the Roman Curia. All cardinals residing in Rome have automatic Vatican citizenship but preserve their original citizenship.

We'll start our tour at the Arch of the Bells in St. Peter's Square. Here visitors can glimpse two of the celebrated Swiss Guards in their colorful uniforms, based on a design by Michelangelo, although the current uniform was actually created in 1928 by one of the Swiss Guard commanders. After the tunnel, on our left we see the Teutonic College and cemetery, the outline of the modern Paul VI audience hall, and the now famous Santa Marta residence-cum-hotel that serves as a home to many prelates who work in the Vatican and to visiting guests and has been home to Pope Francis since his March 13, 2013, election. The cardinal electors stay here during a conclave.

As we go through the quiet streets and paths of Vatican City, our guide will point out the world-famous Mosaic Studio, the Fabric of St. Peter's (the office responsible for the maintenance, upkeep, and repairs of the basilica) and the Scavi Office, where visitors can reserve tours of the pre-Constantine necropolis.

Tours used to stop briefly at the Mosaic Studio, where only a handful of the world's finest artisans repair basilica mosaics, re-create paintings on a made-to-order basis, or execute mosaics commissioned for other churches throughout the world. The studio is no longer on the official itinerary.

A HOLY YEAR IN ROME

The Mosaic Studio boasts a history of almost half a millennium. Its most basic task is to check and restore the 10,000 square meters of mosaic in St. Peter's Basilica. Quite often the artists produce special pieces given by popes as gifts to visitors or when they travel. Since 1847, every papal portrait that adorns the nave of St. Paul Outside-the-Walls Basilica has been done by the Vatican's mosaic workers.

The studio's pride is the invention of *smalti filati*, hair-like filaments that are produced when the fine sticks of enamel are exposed to intense heat. Once, with special permission to visit the artists' workshop, I watched in silence and awe as one of the craftsmen, using the *smalti filati* technique, created the eyelashes of a Madonna. Her eyes were so full of life that I waited for her to blink! This particular technique, using some of the twenty-eight thousand colors catalogued by shades in an immense series of drawers, allows the artists to reproduce with such breathtaking accuracy details such as eyes and eyelashes, folds in garments, strands of hair, the veins in a leaf, the petals of a flower, and even wrinkles in skin.

Continuing our tour, we wend our way to the railway station, whose tracks are measured more in meters than miles. Inaugurated in 1931, it is connected to the Italian railway system and generally used for merchandise delivery, although several popes have used the train to travel to Loreto and Assisi. The magnificent station was converted only a few years ago into a stunning department store where Vatican employees can buy the latest—and the best—in electronic equipment, clothes, jewelry, perfume, handbags, and luggage.

Past the train station, and directly opposite the back of St. Peter's Basilica, is the Governorato, a large building that houses the administrative offices of Vatican City.

It is here that we start what I believe is one of the loveliest parts of the Vatican City visit—my favorite part, in fact—the winding passageways through the incredibly well-manicured and seemingly evergreen Vatican Gardens: the crisscross avenues, lawns, and wooded areas, adorned by artificial caves, monumental statues and fountains, the papal crest done in flowers, a wonderful monument to St. Peter, a shrine to St. Thérèse of Lisieux, the Chinese Pavilion, the Jubilee Bell, and so very much more.

Here and there we spot a bench, an overturned Roman pillar, a fallen bust of ancient times. I always try to imagine popes walking here, alone or in company, praying or trying to solve some of the world's problems. Both John Paul II and Benedict XVI, in fact, loved to walk and pray in the Vatican Gardens.

The Gardens comprise one-third of all Vatican City territory and range from English style to ornate Italian-style gardens, flawless in their beauty and upkeep, thanks to a staff of over two dozen gardeners, to one area that looks as if it has been forgotten for centuries. In a way, I've always liked this seemingly unkempt part the best, for it gives me the feeling of having discovered something, of having gone off the beaten path. I have often explored this part of the Gardens, just to enjoy the immense tranquillity it offers.

Crossing the Gardens we see the Ethiopian College, the Tower of St. John on the highest point of Vatican Hill—where important guests have stayed and where popes have stayed as well when their own apartments were being remodeled—the papal heliport and a replica of the Grotto of Lourdes. The Tower of St. John today houses the offices of the Secretariat for the Economy. Proceeding past the grotto and a basketball court, we come to the famous and much-photographed Rose Garden and the Leonine Tower that once housed the papal observatory. The observatory, by the way, is now at the Papal Palace in Castelgandolfo with its major center and telescope (VATT, Vatican Advanced Telescope Technology) in Tucson, Arizona.

A HOLY YEAR IN ROME

Our route eventually brings us to the mammoth Fountain of the Eagle, whose water, like that of all Vatican fountains, comes from Lake Bracciano, 24 miles north of Rome.

The pièce de résistance is just around the corner, set in a mini-valley. It is a superb architectural jewel known as the Casina Pio IV, "the little house of Pius IV." Begun in 1558, it took four years to build and now houses the Pontifical Academies of Science and Social Sciences. The Casina is actually two buildings facing each other across a marvelous elliptical courtyard. The richly sculpted and painted stucco façades immediately grab your attention, as does the loggia with its fountains and a grotto on the east side. Like everything else within the Vatican walls, it beckons you to closer study and to the enjoyment of its beauty and tranquil setting.

From the Casina you can see the distant Vatican Museums and the Vatican Library—which houses more than eight hundred thousand volumes, eighty thousand manuscripts, ten thousand incunabula, and a hundred thousand etchings—and the Secret Archives, which, I was told on my first visit, have over 60 miles of shelves.

The beauty, history, and splendor of Vatican City State, its buildings, art, and gardens, have been ours for a few brief, magical hours. We've also experienced a remarkable sense of peace. For a fleeting moment, we have left behind the frenetic traffic and chaos of Rome, the crammed buses and piazzas. Peace and serenity envelop us, and we are quite reluctant to leave it.

Now that we have visited Vatican City with its history and the Gardens with their splendor, it's time for the big one! Time to go to the top of St. Peter's Dome. No visit would be complete without an ascent to the cupola, a masterpiece and architectural wonder designed by Michelangelo and completed by Giacomo Della Porta and Domenico Fontana between 1588 and 1590.

Vatican City State

Entrance to the dome is from a courtyard outside the basilica atrium, on the right side. The visitor can ascend to the terrace level of St. Peter's on foot or by elevator. From this point, however, it is all on foot—320 steps in a narrow, winding staircase. There is one stairway up and a separate staircase for descent. Not for the faint of heart—literally—the steep passageways, situated between the two shells of the dome itself, are preceded by warnings for those with physical impairments.

When we have reached the terrace level—this is where we see the huge statues of Christ and the Apostles and saints on the basilica façade—we just follow the signs that say "cupola," and we are on our way to a great adventure. As I said, the staircase is narrow and winding, and we proceed single file. There is *no* turning back once we have started. The ascent is quite literally breathtaking—but so is your reward at the top. The panorama is endless, spellbinding, spectacular! Simultaneously you feel an awesome sense of power and yet one of insignificance: it is like being on the last step of a stairway to heaven.

Well, if you have done it all—toured Vatican City and the Gardens, gone to the *scavi*, visited the museums, the basilica, and the dome—you have spent two days becoming privy to the world of Vatican City State, or at least a fair amount of it. While parts remain off limits to the visitor, much can be seen that tourists are generally not aware of.

You have been surrounded by history, from the depths of the *scavi*, the pre-Constantine necropolis to the soaring heights of St. Peter's Dome. This is a special world and should be visited in a special way.

Forewarned is forearmed: to avoid waiting in long lines, reserve all your Vatican visits *well* in advance of your trip! You can reserve the Vatican Gardens, a tour of the museums and the Sistine

Chapel and the *scavi*, among other fascinating things. As I mentioned earlier, for the *scavi*, you might need to make reservations four to six months before your visit to Rome!

I would set aside two days to visit the Vatican. Allow one morning for the tour of the museums and the Sistine Chapel that you will have reserved in advance. After lunch visit St. Peter's Basilica, with or without a guide. On day 2, take your guided walking tour of Vatican City. Remember, tours are *only* in the morning. Have a leisurely lunch in the nearby Borgo Pio neighborhood, and then take your reserved-well-in-advance tour of the *scavi*.

All the information you need to do so is in the chapter "Joan's Rome: Travel Advice and Tips for Tourists."

Chapter VIII

CASTELGANDOLFO: HISTORY, BEAUTY, AND PEACE MAKE IT A HOME FOR POPES

❖

Roman Pontiffs have spent summers here for centuries, enjoying stupendous panoramas and a climate that is far cooler than Rome's, which can be quite torrid in July and August. Pope John Paul affectionately called it "Vatican Number Two."

I am talking, of course, about the summer papal residence at Castelgandolfo that has a long and colorful history and possesses beauty to rival that of the Apostolic Palace and gardens in Rome.

Castelgandolfo is one of a number of small towns located on beautiful sprawling hills that surround and overlook Lake Albano, about a half-hour drive southeast of Rome. The lake fills an old volcanic crater, is 961 feet above sea level, and is fed by underground sources and drained by an artificial outlet. Lake Albano, said to have been made around 398 B.C., is about two square miles (5 square kilometers) in size and has a maximum depth of 558 feet.

A HOLY YEAR IN ROME

Located on what was once known as Alba Longa, a city in ancient Latium, reputedly the birthplace of Romulus and Remus, Castelgandolfo and the cluster of nearby towns are known as the Alban Hill towns. Romans also call these picturesque towns the Castelli Romani because of the fortified castles originally built on those hills by noble families, around which small towns grew and flourished. Each *castello* bore the name of the lord of the manor.

Castelgandolfo took its name from the Gandulfi family. Originally from Genoa, they built a small square fortress with crenelated walls, an inner courtyard, several towers, and an adjacent garden on the hill where the town that bears their name stands today. The Savelli family later bought the property and owned it until 1596, when, because of a debt they could not pay to Pope Clement VIII (1592-1605), the land became patrimony of the Holy See, forming the nucleus of the papal residence that exists today.

In ensuing centuries, the property underwent many vicissitudes, including the purchase of additional lands, villas, and gardens, and renovations and additions to the original palace. Some of the Roman pontiffs who left their mark on the papal property include Urban VIII (1623-1644); Alexander VII (1655-1667); Clement XI (1700-1721), who bestowed the title "Pontifical Villa" on the property; Benedict XIV (1740); Clement XIII (1758-1769); and Clement XIV (1769-1774).

In 1623 Cardinal Maffeo Barberini was elected Pope, choosing the name Urban VIII (1623-1644). Even before his election, he had spent vacations in Castelgandolfo and had even built a small home near the walls of the original castle/fortress. Once he became Pope, he decided to make this spot his summer residence, readapting and enlarging the old fortress.

One of those who assisted him in this work was the illustrious Carlo Maderno, who, in 1603, after completing the façade of Santa Susanna's Church in Rome, was named as principal architect of the new St. Peter's Basilica. Maderno designed a large wing that overlooked Lake Albano as well as the left part of the façade as seen today from Castelgandolfo's main square. A modest garden was also planted at this time.

Pope Urban VIII moved into the Castelgandolfo residence on May 10, 1626, just six months before the completion of St. Peter's Basilica, following 120 years of work. In 1627, the Pope's nephew, Taddeo Barberini, acquired land and vineyards near the papal residence. Four years later he acquired yet more land and buildings, and the entire complex became known as Villa Barberini. Today this is all an integral part of the pontifical property in Castelgandolfo.

Pope Alexander VII (1655-1667) completed the work begun by Urban VIII, including the long gallery that bears his name, with the assistance of Gian Lorenzo Bernini, noted painter, architect, and sculptor. Interestingly, Bernini also designed part of the gardens of the papal residence, and they can still be seen today.

Bernini is best remembered for having designed the splendid colonnade of 284 pillars that embraces St. Peter's Square, one of the fountains in the square, the basilica's Altar of the Cathedra, the tabernacle in the Blessed Sacrament Chapel, and the baldachin over the central papal altar. Alexander VII also asked Bernini to design the town's parish church, which was named after St. Thomas Villanova.

The nineteenth century saw the unification of Italy, which greatly affected papal holdings, principally the vast Papal States. The Papal States, in fact, under Pope Pius IX were incorporated into the new Italy when the peninsula was unified in 1870. By the by, Pius IX's pontificate from 1846 to 1878 was the second longest in history, following that of St. Peter. From the loss of the

Papal States to the Lateran Pact between Italy and the Holy See on February 11, 1929, under Pius XI, no Pope ever left Vatican City for a holiday in Castelgandolfo.

With the Lateran Treaty, Villa Barberini now belonged to the Holy See and officially became part of the papal residence complex in Castelgandolfo. Pius XI helped to restore the buildings and land that had been unused for so many years. He even bought several orchards in order to set up a small farm to produce goods for consumption in the Vatican and also to underscore the importance of agriculture.

This last acquisition brought the total acreage of the papal property in Castelgandolfo to 136 acres (55 hectares). Vatican City State is 109 acres (44 hectares). In Castelgandolfo, more of the total acreage is dedicated to the farm (62 acres, or 25 hectares) and to gardens than it is to buildings.

The real work of restoration at Castelgandolfo under Pope Pius XI began in 1931. In 1933 the Vatican Observatory, run by the Jesuits, was moved from Vatican City in Rome to Castelgandolfo, because the city lights were too bright for astronomers. The director of the observatory still has an apartment in the palace at Castelgandolfo.

Pius XI also built a new chapel in which he placed a replica of Poland's Black Madonna of Czestochowa. Between 1918 and 1921, he had been, respectively, apostolic visitor and then nuncio in Poland, and had a predilection for the Black Madonna. This chapel has remained unchanged since his day. The Pope's first summer visit was in 1934.

His successor, Pope Pius XII, especially loved Castelgandolfo and spent a great deal of time at this residence, except for the years of World War II. However, during some of the worst moments of the war, Pius allowed the inhabitants of Castelgandolfo and nearby towns to take refuge on the papal property, given that it enjoyed the status of extraterritoriality. After the landing at Anzio in 1944, the citizens of Castelgandolfo were allowed to stay at the Papal Palace, whereas those from other towns were allowed sanctuary in the Villa Barberini property. Pius XII's first postwar visit to the lakeside villa was in 1946. He returned often after that and died there on October 9, 1958.

Pope John XXIII (1958-1963) also enjoyed sojourns at Castelgandolfo. He started two traditions here as Pontiff: praying the Angelus with the faithful on Sundays in the inner courtyard, and celebrating Mass in the parish church of St. Thomas Villanova on August 15, the feast of the Assumption.

Paul VI inaugurated papal trips by helicopter from Castelgandolfo. Continuous use of a helicopter for short papal trips began during the Holy Year of 1975, when Paul VI would return to Rome for the weekly general audiences. He died here on August 6, 1978.

John Paul II, then Cardinal Karol Wojtyla of Krakow, Poland, spent several hours here on October 8, 1978. He returned seventeen days later as Pope, having been elected on October 16. He spent most of every summer here and often came for several days after an especially long and arduous foreign trip.

Benedict XVI also enjoyed the beauty, peace, and subdued rhythm of summer life at Castelgandolfo and spent many summers here for a couple of months following his election to the papacy in April 2005.

Pope Francis has never sojourned at Castelgandolfo but has told Benedict XVI on many occasions he would be more than welcome to stay here. During the summer of 2015, the Pope emeritus did spend two weeks at the Apostolic Palace he so loves.

I earlier mentioned one part of the pontifical property that is called Villa Barberini. Here we find many buildings, including the home of the director of pontifical villas and apartments used by the cardinal secretary of state and by the prefect of the papal household in the summer. The formal gardens, a 62-acre farm, and the remains of Emperor Domitian's (81-96) palatial 14-square-kilometer home are also part of Villa Barberini.

Recently retired as director of the Pontifical Villas at Castelgandolfo, Saverio Petrillo has been serving the Holy See since June 1958. He was named director of the villas in 1986 and authored a book entitled *The Popes at Castelgandolfo*. He was an excellent, knowledgeable, and discreet guide to the papal property and residences.

Dr. Petrillo began his work in Castelgandolfo at the age of eighteen, when he was asked to take the place of a Vatican employee who was ill. In the ensuing years, he has familiarized himself not only with the physical property—the farm, gardens, and buildings—but also with the multicentury history of the villas. His office, as well as other administrative offices, was located in one of the buildings of the Villa Barberini part of the pontifical property and offered splendid views of the Castelli Romani and, in the distance, Rome and the Mediterranean.

Separate from Villa Barberini, but only a short distance away, are the Apostolic Palace and other gardens. The palace—the building overlooking the lake—is where the Pope resides and where the faithful can join him in the courtyard on Sundays for the noon Angelus. At Castelgandolfo, Dr. Petrillo told me on a visit, the Holy Father has the same basic rooms that he has in Rome—a study, a private chapel, a dining room, and a library. The rooms, like the entire palace complex, are on a smaller, more intimate, and homey scale. "Everything here," he said, "is very intimate, warm and family-like. Even the pace of life is slower, more suited to man."

On our tour of the farm, Saverio Petrillo pointed out that it produces eggs, milk (there are twenty-five cows), and yogurt on a daily basis: these are brought early in the morning to the apostolic palaces in both Castelgandolfo and Rome and are sold as well in the Vatican City supermarket under the name Ville Pontificie di Castelgandolfo, "Pontifical Villas of Castelgandolfo." Olive oil is also produced, but in very small quantities. Dr. Petrillo observed that, until a few years ago, Vatican City had its own bakery and also sold fresh fruits and vegetables in its market.

He told me some sixty people work year-round on the papal properties in Castelgandolfo, including gardeners, tree trimmers, those who work at the farm, electricians, other maintenance people, and so forth. Only twenty people permanently reside in buildings on the property.

The heliport, not far from the farm, was first used by Paul VI in 1963, when he visited the cathedral at Orvieto. Continuous use of a helicopter for short papal trips began during the Holy Year of 1975, when Paul VI would return to Rome for the weekly general audiences.

Pope John Paul II, a very athletic Pontiff, asked that a swimming pool be installed at Castelgandolfo to be used for health reasons. Although I did not see the 60-foot-long pool on my tour of the papal villa and gardens, Dr. Petrillo loves to tell the story that when the Pope heard that some people objected to the cost of a pool, he humorously said: "A conclave would cost a lot more." This was John Paul's explanation about how effective physical exercise was in helping him bear the strains of a tiring pontificate.

The beautifully maintained and manicured formal gardens of Villa Barberini have been used by popes through the centuries for long walks and moments of prayer. The flowers, bushes, and trees — of many varieties and trimmed to perfection in geometrical shapes — provide beauty, seclusion and tranquillity. Covering many acres, the stunning formal gardens also provide lovely vistas of the

Roman countryside. There are statues, fountains, and a labyrinth of walkways and roads, one of which dates to Roman times and is paved exactly like the Old Appian Way.

One olive tree in the gardens has a special story. Just an olive branch at the time, it was given by King Hussein of Jordan to Pope Paul VI during his trip to Jerusalem in 1964. The late king's son and heir, now King Abdullah, was able to visit the gardens and saw the fully grown tree.

Ruins of Emperor Domitian's villa can be found everywhere, and occasionally one will see a niche with a statue from the villa.

Domitian, who ruled from 81 to 96, had built a 14-square-kilometer villa and garden area on this site. It was constructed on three levels: the top floor of the villa was for the servants, the middle was for the imperial family and their guests, and the bottom was the crypto-portico, which is in near perfect condition nearly two thousand years later. The crypto-portico, reached now by a staircase built into the gardens, was constructed to provide the emperor and his guests with a cool place to walk, talk, and sit to escape from the summer heat of Rome. Enormous in size, it resembles a tunnel—with one end open and the other closed. The closed end has a raised stagelike level, accessible by a staircase: today there is a large cross here. The ceiling is curved and, on the western wall, there are windows at the top level. Dr. Petrillo said these were once covered with alabaster to let in the late-afternoon sunlight—but not the heat.

Also at Villa Barberini is the Antiquarium, a museum that houses a small but prized collection of artifacts from Domitian's villa that were discovered over the past century. Only restricted numbers of scholars are allowed to visit the Antiquarium, which includes busts, statues, columns, portals, and tables made of marble and various stones, to mention but a few objects.

Castelgandolfo

On September 11, 2015, the Vatican announced a new "Full Day in the Vatican" tour that includes the Vatican Museums and Gardens and a train trip to Castelgandolfo and the Papal Palace. For complete information, see "Four Special Tours from the Vatican Museums Website" in chapter 12.

Chapter IX

AND IF YOU
HAVE TIME ...

$$\diamondsuit$$

I would be terribly remiss if I did not take a few moments to mention just a few of the other churches in Rome that would, taken individually, merit almost as much attention as we have given to the seven basilicas. All of the churches I am about to list are noted for their place in history, their architectural beauty, and as repositories of some of the greatest works of art that man has ever known. Many are shrines in their own right as they house the bodies or relics of numerous pontiffs and saints.

If you have the time on this trip—or plan to come back to Rome—make sure they are on your itinerary. Most are within a half-mile radius of the center of Rome. Should you be staying in or near the center, you can visit many of them.

If you are coming from Vatican City, you will cross the Tiber and walk down Corso Vittorio Emanuele, heading toward Piazza Venezia. On your left is Santa Maria della Vallicella (St. Mary's in the Little Valley), also known as the Chiesa Nuova. The principal church of the Oratorians, founded by St. Philip Neri, the first church on this site was built by St. Gregory the Great. By the twelfth century, it was known as Santa Maria della Vallicella. In 1575 Pope Gregory XIII recognized the Oratorians as a congregation and gave them this church. The church was rebuilt, starting that same year. St. Philip is buried in a chapel to the left of the main altar in a tomb decorated with mother-of-pearl. The main altarpiece was done by Rubens.

Continuing along the Corso, on your right you will come to the Church of Sant'Andrea della Valle (St. Andrew of the Valley), begun late in the sixteenth century, whose original façade was by Maderno. The Baroque façade by Carlo Rainaldi was added between 1655 and 1663. Sant'Andrea's dome was for a long time the third largest in Rome after St. Peter's and the Pantheon. If its interior seems familiar to you, this church was chosen by Giacomo Puccini as the scene for the first act of his opera *Tosca*. This basilica is the general seat for the Theatine Congregation. The fresco decorations were one of the largest such commissions of the time. Popes Pius II and Pius III (whose papacy was one of the shortest ever, from September 22 to October 18, 1503) are buried here.

Exiting Sant'Andrea, we proceed straight ahead, to Corso Rinascimento. Halfway up, turn left onto the elegant Piazza Navona, often called "Rome's living room," where you will find the Church of Sant'Agnese (St. Agnes), one of Francesco Borromini's wonderful works. The church was consecrated on January 17, 1672, and is dedicated to Agnes, a young Roman girl who was martyred at the age of thirteen in what today is Piazza Navona but was once the ancient elliptical stadium of the emperor Domitian, which could hold thirty thousand spectators. Opposite the church—in the center of this extraordinary piazza—is the most famous of the three fountains that decorate this square—Bernini's Fountain of the Four Rivers (the Nile, Ganges, Rio de la Plata, and Danube).

And If You Have Time ...

Behind the Church of St. Agnes on Via Santa Maria dell'Anima are two much-loved churches: Santa Maria dell'Anima, the German national church in Rome, with a sixteenth-century façade by Sangallo and windows by Bramante, and Santa Maria della Pace (St. Mary of Peace), a jewel of a church built in 1480, with paintings by Raphael and Caravaggio. Attached to it is a cloister built by Bramante in 1504.

Returning to Piazza Navona, we walk to the eastern end — to our right as we look at the Church of St. Agnes. We exit here, turn right, cross the street, and walk under the archway linking two buildings. On our left is the Church of San Agostino (St. Augustine), built over the previous church on that site, commissioned in 1350 by Cardinal Guillaume d'Estouteville. Raphael's *Isaiah* can be found on the third pillar on the left of the nave. In the chapel by the exit is a Caravaggio masterpiece, *The Madonna of the Pilgrims*, painted in 1609.

Still in the vicinity of Piazza Navona is the Church of San Luigi dei Francesi (St. Louis of the French), the French national church, begun in 1618. This church was designed by Giacomo della Porta (the façade is by della Porta) and built by Domenico Fontana between 1518 and 1589. San Luigi is most famous for the cycle of paintings on the life of St. Matthew by Caravaggio, the Baroque master, in the Contarelli Chapel.

Only a short walk from Navona we find the Pantheon in the piazza of the same name. This imposing edifice was built by Emperor Marco Agrippa in A.D. 27 as a temple to the gods (*pantheon* comes from the Greek, meaning "many gods"). Now a Catholic Church, where Raphael as well as the former kings and queens of Italy are buried, it is noteworthy for its dome, whose diameter — 43.3 meters — is the same as its highest point from the floor. The dome has a single, circular opening at the apex called the oculus. On Pentecost Sunday, after the 10:30 a.m. Mass, tens of thousands of red rose petals are released into the church from the oculus by Roman firemen. Red is the color for Pentecost, and the petals symbolize the Holy Spirit coming down on the faithful, a modern-day echo of the Holy Spirit's descending on the Apostles on the first Pentecost.

Just a few feet away from the Pantheon is the Church of Santa Maria sopra Minerva (St. Mary over Minerva), built over a temple to Minerva. Located on the Via del Beato Angelico at Piazza Minerva, it is the only Gothic-style church in Rome. It is renowned for Fra Filippo Lippi's masterpiece *St. Thomas Presenting Cardinal Carafa to the Blessed Virgin*, located over the altar in the main chapel of the transept. The remains of St. Catherine of Siena, who was influential in bringing the papacy back to Rome after its years of exile in Avignon (1309-1377), rest below the main altar. To the left of this altar is a work by Michelangelo, *Christ Carrying His Cross*. In a chapel on the left, beneath a perpetually burning light, are the remains of Fra Giovanni da Fiesole, better known as Fra Angelico. Often called the greatest sacred painter of Christianity, Fra Angelico died in 1455. In front of the church, and almost equally as famous, is the marble elephant sculpted by Gian Lorenzo Bernini in 1667, at the base of a small obelisk.

As we exit this church, we take the street to our left, Via dei Cestari, which will bring us to Largo Argentina and back to Corso Vittorio Emanuele. A two-minute walk up the Corso brings us to the Church of Gesù (Jesus), the mother church of the Society of Jesus (the Jesuits), which is a lavish example of what has come to be called the Jesuit style. One of its most precious works of art is a cenotaph (a monument dedicated to a person who is buried elsewhere) to St. Robert Bellarmine, featuring a bust of the saint by Bernini. The idea for this church was first conceived in 1551 by St. Ignatius of Loyola, founder of the Jesuits. The Gesù was home to the superior general of the order until it was suppressed in 1773. It now has an adjacent residence for Jesuit scholars from around the world who come to study at the celebrated Jesuit-run Gregorian University.

Proceeding up Corso Vittorio, we arrive at Piazza Venezia. We turn right, walk to the corner, and on our right is the delightful and beautiful Church of San Marco (St. Mark), founded in 336 by Pope St. Mark in honor of the Evangelist, who is buried in St. Mark's Church in Venice. In the fifteenth century Pope Paul II ordered this to be the church of Venetians in Rome. It features the tombstone of Vannozza de' Cattani, the mother of Lucrezia, Cesare, Giofre, and Giovanni Borgia.

Remaining in the center of Rome, we now go to San Ignazio (St. Ignatius), another Jesuit church. A five-minute walk from Piazza Venezia, just off Via del Corso at Via Caravita, brings us to Piazza San Ignazio. Construction of the church, with its sumptuous Baroque façade, began in 1626, four years after the canonization of St. Ignatius Loyola, who founded the Society of Jesus in 1534. A lapis-lazuli urn under the elegant altar of the right transept contains the remains of St. Aloysius Gonzaga, an Italian Jesuit and patron of youth.

Now, let's return to Via del Corso and proceed north to Piazza del Popolo, where we will visit Santa Maria del Popolo (St. Mary of the People), one of two churches on either side of Via del Corso as it enters this lovely nineteenth-century square. The fifteenth-century church is celebrated for two masterpieces by Caravaggio, *The Conversion of St. Paul* and *The Crucifixion of St. Peter*. The first chapel on the right, dedicated to the Della Rovere family, was frescoed by Pinturicchio, and the Chigi Chapel, on the left aisle, features a rare architectural work by Raphael, which caused many to remark that his greater talent by far was that of a painter! Above the main altar is a painting of a Madonna attributed to St. Luke.

Reversing our direction, we'll now take Via del Corso to Piazza Venezia, then up the Fori Imperiali and past the Roman Forum. In the area of the Coliseum, on the Oppian Hill, is San Pietro in Vincoli (St. Peter in Chains), rebuilt over an early church by the priest Philip on his return from the Council of Ephesus in 431. Eight years later, it was consecrated and dedicated to Sts. Peter and Paul, although the name it has today dates back to the sixth century. The church is renowned for the relics of the chains that bound St. Peter when he was imprisoned in Rome, and for one of Michelangelo's most memorable sculptures, *Moses*.

Next on our itinerary is the Basilica of San Clemente (St. Clement), just minutes away from St. John Lateran, and definitely worth a detour when you are in the area. One of the best preserved medieval basilicas in Rome, it rests over a fourth-century church that was destroyed in 1084. Entering from Via San Giovanni, we find a chapel with frescoes that occupy an important place in church art. At the center of the nave is the marvelous *schola cantorum* of the earlier basilica, a wonderful cosmatesque floor, and two exceptional ambones (you will remember the ambones, the two pulpits for the Epistle and the Gospel, which we saw in St. Lawrence Outside-the-Walls). From the sacristy one descends into the lower basilica, noted for its wonderful frescoes of the eleventh and twelfth centuries, and a few from the second half of the ninth century. Still below this are the underlying Roman constructions from the imperial period.

East of Rome's center, on the Via Nomentana, we find the Basilica of Sant'Agnese (St. Agnes), also called St. Agnes Outside-the-Walls, which was erected in 342 by Constantine's daughter, Constantia, in memory of this young martyr, who died defending her chastity and her faith. The relics of St. Agnes, and those of St. Emerentiana, lie in a beautiful silver reliquary. The basilica complex includes the Mausoleum of St. Constantia, built by Constantine as a funeral monument for his daughters, and the catacombs of St. Agnes.

A particularly wonderful story is linked to this church, so allow me to digress a bit at this point.

In keeping with the tradition for the feast of St. Agnes (January 21), two baby lambs, blessed earlier in the morning in the Roman basilica named for this saint, are brought to the Vatican and the papal apartments. The lambs are raised by the Trappist Fathers of the Abbey of the Three Fountains. When their wool is shorn, the Sisters of St. Cecilia weave it into the palliums (plural is occasionally *pallia*) that, on the feast of Sts. Peter and Paul (June 29), are given to new metropolitan archbishops as signs of their office. Once the palliums are made, they are stored in a coffer in the Niche of the Palliums, right below the main altar of St. Peter's in the area we saw called the Confessio. They are removed from the niche on the eve of the ceremony.

The pallium is a white woolen circular band embroidered with six black crosses that is worn over the shoulders and has two hanging pieces, one in front and another in back. Worn by the Pope and by metropolitan archbishops, it symbolizes authority and expresses the special bond between the bishops and the Roman Pontiff.

In a 1978 document, *Inter Eximina Episcopalis*, Pope Paul VI restricted its use to the Pope and metropolitan archbishops. Six years later, Pope John Paul decreed that it be conferred on the metropolitans by the Pope on the feast of Sts. Peter and Paul. In yet another change, Pope Francis decreed that the pallium be given to each metropolitan privately on June 29 by the Pope but be actually placed on the archbishop's shoulders in his home diocese by the nuncio to the country involved.

Usually in attendance at the January 21 ceremony in the Vatican are two Trappist fathers, several nuns, two canons of the Chapter of St. John, the dean of the Roman Rota, two officials from the Office of the Liturgical Celebrations of the Supreme Pontiff, and a number of other invited guests. By tradition, the guest list is always twenty-one people.

The baby lambs, under a year of age, are normally tucked in wicker baskets, and both lambs and baskets are adorned with flowers. In 2004 venerable Pope John Paul II blessed the lambs during a general audience in the Paul VI Hall, as both the audience and St. Agnes's feast day occurred on a Wednesday.

As we said, Agnes died about 305 and is buried in the basilica named for her on Rome's Via Nomentana. Historical accounts vary about the birth, life, and manner of death of Agnes, but generally it is recounted that, in order to preserve her virginity, she was martyred at a very young age, probably twelve. She is usually depicted with a lamb because the Latin word so similar to her name, *agnus*, means "lamb." The name Agnes is actually derived from the feminine Greek adjective *hagnē* meaning "chaste" or "pure."

Now, let's resume our tour of some of Rome's countless beautiful and historical churches.

Back in the center of Rome is the Church of Santa Maria degli Angeli (St. Mary of the Angels), located on Piazza della Repubblica, not far from the Termini rail station. Once the baths of the emperor Diocletian—and we can see some of the ruins nearby—this was transformed into the grandiose church it is today by Michelangelo. It has a colossal transept and is decorated by eight monolithic red granite columns from the original baths.

And If You Have Time ...

The last churches we'll see are in two parts of the city we have not yet visited, the Aventine Hill, and Trastevere.

The elegant Aventine neighborhood overlooks the Circus Maximus and the Baths of Caracalla. Situated in the Piazza Pietro d'Illyria, the Basilica of Santa Sabina (St. Sabina) was established at the start of the fifth century by a priest named Peter who was from Illyria. In 1222 Pope Honorius III gave the adjacent ancient turreted palace of the Crescenzi family to the Dominicans as a monastery, and, in fact, over the years both Sts. Dominic and Thomas Aquinas lived here. Modifications and additions to the sixteenth-century basilica altered its appearance. In the early 1900s, the church was restored to its original design. It has three aisles and twenty-four fluted Corinthian columns. Little is left of the original mosaics. In the middle of the nave is the mosaic tombstone dedicated to Munoz de Zamora, master general of the Dominicans and a biographer of St. Dominic. Adjacent to the church is the cloister built by St. Dominic in 1220 and restored between 1936 and 1939.

Close by is the Benedictine Abbey of San Anselmo. Every year on Ash Wednesday, the Pope processes from St. Anselm's to St. Sabina's, where he receives ashes. St. Sabina's, by the way, is, and has been for many centuries, one of the primary station churches in Rome during the Lenten season.

We close with a visit to Santa Maria in Trastevere (St. Mary's in Trastevere), located in one of the oldest and most colorful neighborhoods in the Eternal City. Dating from the twelfth century, St. Mary's is located in the square by the same name. Its façade, modified in 1702 and based on a design by Maderno, features a beautiful bell tower and mosaics. It has three aisles, divided by twenty-one Ionic columns from pagan buildings and has its original cosmatesque floor. The first church built here dates from Pope

St. Calixtus (217-222) who, it is said, built it on a spot where, in the year 38 B.C., a prodigious eruption of oil occurred, interpreted as pre-announcing the arrival of the Messiah. Julius I (337-352) rebuilt the church in the form of a basilica. It was again modified in the eighth and ninth centuries.

Chapter X

JUBILEE OF MERCY CALENDAR OF EVENTS

— ❖ —

Following is the May 5, 2015, presentation by Archbishop Rino Fisichella, president of the Pontifical Council for Promoting the New Evangelization, the council charged with organizing the Jubilee of Mercy. He explains some of the details of the official calendar of events for this Jubilee Year:

> The Apostolic Exhortation *Evangelii Gaudium*, which continues to be the programmatic outline for the pontificate of Pope Francis, offers a meaningful expression of the very essence of the Extraordinary Jubilee announced on April 11: "Such a community [the Church] has an endless desire to show mercy, the fruit of its own experience of the power of the Father's infinite mercy. Let us try a little harder to take the first step and to become involved" (EG 24). It is with this desire in mind that we should re-read the Bull of Indiction of the Jubilee, *Misericordiae vultus*, in which Pope

A HOLY YEAR IN ROME

Francis details the aims of the Holy Year. As you know, the two dates already marked out are December 8 , the Solemnity of the Immaculate Conception—the day of the opening of the Holy Door of Saint Peter's Basilica—and November 20, 2016 , the Solemnity of Our Lord Jesus Christ, King of the Universe, which will conclude the Holy Year. Between these two dates a calendar of various events is being developed.

In order to avoid any misunderstanding, it is important to reiterate that this Jubilee of Mercy is not and does not intend to be the Great Jubilee Year of 2000. Therefore, any comparisons lack validity, for every Holy Year possesses its own unique nature and aims. It is the Pope's desire that this Jubilee be celebrated in Rome as well as in the local Churches; this will give due focus to the life of individual Churches and their needs, in such a way that the initiatives will not place an extra burden on local Churches, but will blend into their calendars and usual activities very naturally. Also, for the first time in the history of the Jubilee tradition, there will be an opportunity for individual dioceses to open a Holy Door—The Door of Mercy—either in the Cathedral or in a church of special meaning or a shrine of particular importance for pilgrimages.

Similarly, it is easy to cull other characteristics from the Bull of Indiction that will make this Jubilee unique. From the very beginning, however, the call to mercy breaks with the traditional pattern. The history of Jubilees has been marked by their occurrence every fifty or twenty-five years. The two extraordinary Jubilees fell on anniversaries of Christ's redemptive act (1933, 1983). This Jubilee, however, is based upon a theme.

It will build upon the central content of the faith and intends to call the Church once again to its missionary priority of being a sign and witness in every aspect of its pastoral life. I also have in mind Pope Francis's appeal to Judaism and Islam as loci in which to contextualize the theme of mercy in order to foster dialogue and a way of overcoming difficulties in the public realm.

We must also not forget another original characteristic of this Jubilee—namely, the designation of *Missionaries of Mercy*. Pope Francis will give them their mandate on Ash Wednesday during the celebration in St. Peter's Basilica. The Missionaries must be patient priests, possessing an understanding of human frailty but ready to express the loving kindness of the Good Shepherd in their preaching and in the sacrament of Confession. However, I would rather not spend too much time on these general questions, because it is important now to explain some of the specifics pertaining to the organization of the Holy Year.

We begin with the logo, which represents a summa theologiae of the theme of mercy and the motto that accompanies it. The motto Merciful Like the Father (taken from Luke 6:36) serves as an invitation to follow the merciful example of the Father, who asks us not to judge or condemn but to forgive and to give love and forgiveness without measure (cf. Luke 6:37-38). The logo is the work of Father Marko I. Rupnik. It shows an image quite important to the early Church: that of the Son having taken upon His shoulders the lost soul, demonstrating that it is the love of Christ that brings to completion the mystery of His Incarnation, culminating in redemption. The logo has been designed in such a way as to express the profound way in which the Good Shepherd touches the flesh of humanity and does so with a love that has the power to change one's life. One particular feature worthy of note is that while the Good Shepherd, in His great mercy, takes humanity upon Himself, His eyes are merged with those of man. Christ sees with the eyes of Adam, and Adam with the eyes of Christ. Every person discovers in Christ, the new Adam, his own humanity and the future that lies ahead. The three concentric ovals, with colors progressively lighter as we move outward, suggest the movement of Christ, who carries humanity out of the darkness of sin and death. Conversely, the depth of the darker color suggests the impenetrability of the love of the Father, who forgives all. The logo has been registered in the international forum in order to safeguard its rights and to prevent any inappropriate use. It is obvious that permission must be granted by the Pontifical Council for any nonreligious use of the logo and that any abuses will be duly dealt with.

The *calendar of celebrations* is to be read from three perspectives. First, some events are being organized which most likely will involve large crowds of people. We wanted the first event, which will be held from January 19-21, to be dedicated to all those involved with the organization of pilgrimages. It will symbolically emphasize that the Holy Year is a true pilgrimage and should be lived as such. We will ask pilgrims to make a journey on foot, preparing themselves to pass through the Holy Door in a spirit of faith and devotion. It will be essential to prepare those working in the travel industry sector to go beyond the sphere of tourism, because they will be the first to provide assistance to pilgrims.

We thought it would be important to gather together believers who live in a particular way the experience of mercy. It is for this reason that, on April 3, we will have a celebration for those who in various ways are inspired by a charism of mercy (movements, associations, and religious institutes). On September 4, *charitable volunteers* will gather from all over the world. A volunteer is a dynamic witness of someone who lives the works of mercy in its various expressions and deserves to be celebrated in this special way. Similarly, for those who are inspired in a particular way by *Mary*, there will be a special day on October 9 to celebrate her as the *Mother of Mercy*.

There will be a number of events dedicated particularly to *youth*, who upon receiving the Sacrament of Confirmation are called to profess their faith. For those between the ages of 13 and 16, for whom there are few opportunities for involvement within the ordinary pastoral life of the Church, we have reserved the date of April 24, as World Youth Day, which will be held in Krakow from July 26-31 and is geared toward youth of an older age bracket.

Another event will be for *deacons* who by their vocation and ministry are called to preside in works of charity in the life of the Christian community. Their Jubilee will be held on May 29. On June 3, which marks the 160th anniversary of the Feast of the Sacred Heart of Jesus, there will be a Jubilee celebration for *priests*. On September 25 there will be the Jubilee of *catechists* who, in transmitting the life of faith, support Christian communities and, in particular, our parishes in a decisive way. On June 12, we will have a large gathering for the *sick and disabled*, as well as for those who care for them with such love and dedication.

A HOLY YEAR IN ROME

On November 6, we will celebrate the Jubilee for *those in prison*. This will be held not only in prisons but we have been studying the possibility of giving many of those in prison the opportunity to celebrate their own Holy Year with Pope Francis in St. Peter's Basilica.

Secondly, there will be significant efforts to enact Pope Francis's vision and witness of reaching out to those on the existential "peripheries" of society, in order to give a direct testimony to the Church's affinity and care for the poor, the suffering, the marginalized, and all those who need a sign of tenderness. These moments will have a symbolic meaning, but we will also ask bishops and priests to perform in their own dioceses similar symbolic gestures of communion with Pope Francis so that everyone may receive a concrete sign of the Church's ministry of mercy and closeness. As a concrete sign of the Pope's charitable love, which is an essential component of this Jubilee, effective measures will be taken to meet real needs in the world that will express mercy through tangible assistance.

Thirdly, we must meet the needs of the many pilgrims who will come alone to Rome apart from any organized tour or tour group. For these individuals, there will be a number of churches in the historic center of Rome where they will feel welcome, where they can have moments of reflective prayer and prepare themselves thoroughly to walk through the Holy Door in an atmosphere of genuine spiritual devotion. All the pilgrims who will come to Rome, however, will have a privileged route through which to walk through the Holy Door. This is necessary in order to ensure that the event is lived in a religious way, safe from any climate of abuse that can easily confront millions of people making a pilgrimage to Christian holy sites.

The official website for the Jubilee has already been launched: *www.iubilaeummisericordiae.va* and can also be accessed at www.im.va. The site is available in seven languages: Italian, English, Spanish, Portuguese, French, German, and Polish. On the site you will find official information regarding the calendar of the major public events, information for participating in the events with the Holy Father, and all of the official communications regarding the Jubilee. Also, through the site, dioceses will be able to receive information and pastoral suggestions, register pilgrimage groups, and relay to us their local diocesan projects. The website uses a number of social networks (Facebook, Twitter, Instagram, Google Plus, and Flickr) through which we will be able to provide updates on the Holy Father's initiative and follow in real time the major events as they take place. We have also been studying the possibility of an app with which to better integrate all this information.

We are convinced that the path of Mercy on which Pope Francis has placed the Church in this journey of the Jubilee will be a moment of true grace for all Christians and a reawaking to the path of the new evangelization and the pastoral conversion the Pope has indicated. As Pope Francis wrote: "In this Jubilee Year, may the Church echo the word of God that resounds strong and clear as a message and a sign of pardon, strength, aid, and love. May she never tire of extending mercy, and be ever patient in offering compassion and comfort. May the Church become the voice of every man and woman, and repeat confidently without end: 'Be mindful of your mercy, O Lord, and your steadfast love, for they have been from of old'" (MV 25).

✦

CALENDAR OF CELEBRATIONS

April 2015	
Saturday, April 11 *Vigil for Divine Mercy Sunday*	Reading of the Bolla (Bull) of Indiction of the Jubilee

December 2015	
Tuesday, December 8 *Solemnity of the Immaculate Conception*	Opening of the Holy Door of St. Peter's Basilica
Sunday, December 13 *Third Sunday of Advent*	Opening of the Holy Door of the Basilica of St. John Lateran and in the Cathedrals of the world

Jubilee of Mercy Calendar of Events

January 2016

Friday, January 1
Solemnity of Mary, the Holy Mother of God and World Day for Peace

Opening of the Holy Door of the Basilica of Saint Mary Major

Tuesday through Thursday, January 19 through 21

Jubilee for those Engaged in Pilgrimage Work

Monday, January 25
Feast of the Conversion of St. Paul

Opening of the Holy Door of the Basilica of St. Paul Outside-the-Walls

"Jubilee" sign of the Holy Father: witness of the works of mercy

February 2016

Tuesday, February 2
Feast of the Presentation of the Lord and the Day for Consecrated Life

Jubilee for Consecrated Life and the closing of the Year for Consecrated Life

Monday through Sunday, February 8 through 14

The remains of St. Pio of Pietrelcina (Padre Pio) will be exposed for veneration in St. Peter's Basilica.

Wednesday, February 10 *Ash Wednesday*	Sending forth of the Missionaries of Mercy, St. Peter's Basilica
Monday, February 22 *Feast of the Chair of St. Peter*	Jubilee for the Roman Curia "Jubilee" sign of the Holy Father: witness of the works of mercy

March 2016

Friday and Saturday, March 4 and 5	"24 Hours for the Lord" with a penitential liturgy in St. Peter's Basilica on the afternoon of Friday, March 4
Sunday, March 20 *Palm Sunday*	The diocesan World Day for Youth in Rome "Jubilee" sign of the Holy Father: witness of the works of mercy

April 2016

Sunday, April 3 *Divine Mercy Sunday*	Jubilee for those who are devoted to the spirituality of Divine Mercy

Sunday, April 24 *Fifth Sunday of Easter*	Jubilee for boys and girls (ages 13 to 16) "Jubilee" sign of the Holy Father: witness of the works of mercy

May 2016

Sunday through Tuesday, May 27 through 29 *Solemnity of Corpus Christi in Italy*	Jubilee for deacons

June 2016

Friday, June 3 *Solemnity of the Most Sacred Heart of Jesus*	Jubilee for priests 160 years since the introduction of this feast by Pope Pius IX in 1856
Sunday, June 12 *Eleventh Sunday in Ordinary Time*	Jubilee for those who are ill and for persons with disabilities "Jubilee" sign of the Holy Father: witness of the works of mercy

July 2016

Tuesday through Sunday, July 26 through 31
(*to conclude on the Eighteenth Sunday in Ordinary Time*)

Jubilee for young people

World Youth Day in Krakow, Poland

September 2016

Sunday, September 4
Twenty-Third Sunday in Ordinary Time

Jubilee for workers and volunteers of mercy

Memorial of Blessed Teresa of Calcutta (September 5)

Sunday, September 25
Twenty-Sixth Sunday in Ordinary Time

Jubilee for catechists

October 2016

Saturday and Sunday, October 8 and 9
(*Saturday and Sunday after the Memorial of Our Lady of the Rosary*)

Marian Jubilee

November 2016

Tuesday, November 1 *Solemnity of All Saints*	Holy Mass celebrated by the Holy Father in memory of the faithful departed
Sunday, November 6 *Thirty-Second Sunday in Ordinary Time*	In St. Peter's Basilica, the Jubilee for prisoners
Sunday, November 13 *Thirty-Third Sunday in Ordinary Time*	Closing of the Holy Doors in the Basilicas of Rome and in the Dioceses of the world
Sunday, November 20 *Solemnity of Our Lord Jesus Christ, King of the Universe*	Closing of the Holy Door of St. Peter's Basilica and the conclusion of the Jubilee of Mercy

Chapter XI

JOAN'S ROME: TRAVEL ADVICE

❖

On my blog, *Joan's Rome*, there is a link entitled "Practical Information on Visiting the Vatican" (http://www.ewtn.com/saintsHoly/visit_vatican.asp). This gives you tons of information about visiting the Vatican, but I also add some notes about restaurants and hotels in Rome, and so forth. I put these notes together because, as you might imagine, I receive countless requests for information about tours, how to visit the Vatican, places to stay in Rome and Italy, and so forth. Because there is no way I can personally answer the many letters and individual requests, I prepared these tips for tourists for people planning to visit Rome and the Vatican at any time but especially during the December 8, 2015, to November 20, 2016, Jubilee Year of Mercy. My tips do not include such practical information as buying bus tickets, getting around Rome, exchanging money, and so forth. Your tour guide or hotel staff, or both, can help you on most of these matters.

In addition to the information below on reserving tickets for the Vatican Museums, tours of the Vatican Gardens, and visits to the world-famous *scavi*, and so forth, I highly recommend the following helpful websites:

www.santasusanna.org

http://www.vaticanstate.va/EN/_Practical_Informations.htm

http://www.pnac.org/general/visiting_vatican.htm

PRACTICAL INFORMATION FOR VISITING THE VATICAN

(from the www.vaticanstate.va link above)

AUDIENCES. A ticket—always free of charge—is required for attending the General Audience on Wednesday mornings or other ceremonies. They are issued by the Prefecture of the Papal Household and you will be told where to pick them up in the prefecture's response to your request for tickets. Usually the ticket pickup office is accessed by way of the Bronze Door (Portone di Bronzo). The office is open Mondays from 9 a.m. to 1 p.m. and Tuesdays from 9 a.m. to 6 p.m. The website is: http://www.vatican.va/various/prefettura/index_en.html.

To request a ticket: Fax +39.06.69885863.

A note from Joan: Remember, you can also ask for tickets through the North American College (NAC) by going to the website of the Visitors Office of the Pontifical North American College (www.pnac.org/general/visiting_vatican.htm) or by visiting www.santasusanna.org, the church in Rome for Americans that, like NAC, on Tuesday afternoons distributes tickets to those who have requested them in advance. They can be picked up at the Paulist Fathers' office, and that information is on their website. I recommend both of these avenues because of the extraordinarily personal treatment you will receive as you meet fellow Americans, "ex-pat" Americans who live in Rome.

ST. PETER'S BASILICA. The Basilica is open every day from 7 a.m. to 7 p.m., April through September and from 7 a.m. to 6 p.m., October through March. To preserve the sacred character of the church, groups consisting of more than five members and accompanied by a guide are kindly requested to use "audio-guides," which can be rented at the entrance to the basilica. Proper dress is required for admission to the basilica. To rent "audio-guides," telephone +39.06.69883229 or +39.06.69881898.

A note from Joan: "Proper dress" means that knees and shoulders must be covered—for men and women.

P.S. To get into the basilica without waiting in a long line, go to the 8:30 a.m. Mass in the Blessed Sacrament Chapel, on the right aisle of the basilica. This way you have the beauty of Mass and the joy of experiencing this marvelous basilica without the tourists, as tourists are not allowed in until 9 a.m. As you line up for security, tell the guards you are going to Mass (*la Messa*). If you cannot make Mass, but want to visit the basilica when it opens at 9 a.m., try to be in line for security by about 8:30.

HISTORICAL AND ARTISTIC MUSEUM (TREASURY). The Treasury is open from 9 a.m. to 6:15 p.m., April through September and from 9 a.m. to 5:15 p.m., October through March. The entrance is from inside St. Peter's Basilica (on the left side).

A HOLY YEAR IN ROME

VISIT TO THE DOME. Visits to the dome of St. Peter's are possible every day from 8 a.m. to 6 p.m., April through September, and from 8 a.m. to 5 p.m., October through March. The entrance is at the portico of the basilica (on the right-hand side of the basilica, just off the atrium).

> A note from Joan: There are 320 steps to the top of the dome, and it is an incredibly wonderful experience but also—and literally—breathtaking! Anyone with heart ailments, breathing problems, or anything else that might be a serious impediment to scaling that height is forewarned before taking even one step. You can't go a quarter of the way, for example, and decide it is too much and turn around. It is all or nothing! The staircase is wide enough for only a single person.

VATICAN GROTTOES. The Vatican Grottoes are open every day from 9am to 6pm, April through September, and from 9 a.m. to 5 p.m., October through March. Masses are celebrated daily in the grotto area from 7 a.m. to 9 a.m. when the basilica opens, and access is granted only to those who have an invitation to a Mass or are with a specific group accompanied by a priest. The entrance is at the transept of St. Peter's Basilica.

VISIT TO THE TOMB OF ST. PETER AND THE PRE-CONSTANTINIAN NECROPOLIS. For visits to the tomb of St. Peter and the necropolis (known as the scavi, meaning "excavations"), please contact the Ufficio Scavi (excavations office): tel. + 39.06.69885318; fax + 39.06 698 73017; e-mail: scavi@fsp.va. The office is open from 9 a.m. to 5 p.m., Monday through Friday, and reached by way of the Arch of the Bells. For full information on scavi tickets and tours: http://www.vatican.

va/roman_curia/institutions_connected/uffscavi/documents/
rc_ic_uffscavi_doc_gen-information_20040112_en.html

A note from Joan: This is one of the best visits you will make in Rome—or perhaps all of Italy—*but* you *must* book well in advance. Several months before your departure is *not* too early to request a *scavi* visit.

VISIT TO THE VATICAN MUSEUMS. The Vatican Museums are open weekdays from 10 a.m. to 1:45 p.m. from November through February (except during the Christmas period, when they are open from 8:45 a.m. to 4:45 p.m.). From March through October the museums are open Monday through Friday from 10 a.m. to 4:45 p.m. and Saturdays from 10 a.m. to 2:45 p.m. On the last Sunday of each month the museums can be visited free of admission from 9 a.m. to 1:45 p.m. Entrance to the museums is not possible 75 minutes before closing time. There are also Friday evening visits during the summer, so check the Vatican Museums website.

The ticket office is open Monday to Saturday from 9 a.m to 4 p.m. The Museums close at 6 p.m. N.B.: Exit from rooms half an hour before closing time. Museums are closed on the following days: January 1, 6; February 11; March 19; Easter Sunday and Easter Monday; May 1; June 29 (Sts. Peter and Paul); August 15: December 8, 25, 26.

Book in advance online: http://www.museivaticani.va/3_EN/pages/MV_Home.html.

For information, telephone +39.06.69883860 or fax +39.06.69885433

To arrange *advanced* bookings for guided tours:
e-mail visiteguidate.musei@scv.va
telephone +39.06.69884676 (for individuals)

A HOLY YEAR IN ROME

telephone +39.06.69883145 (for groups)

fax +39.06.69883578

Four special tours from the Vatican Museums website (reservations are required for all three visits: http://mv.vatican.va/3_EN/ pages/MV_Home.html).

As of March 1, 2014, pilgrims and tourists have been able to visit the Pontifical Villa of Castelgandolfo, the summer papal residence, and the exclusive Barberini Gardens. Accompanied by a multilingual guide, visitors will have access to the botanical and architectural wonders of the pontifical residence, also known as "Vatican Two."

The Vatican Museums also offer special seasonal appointments in the form of the Friday Night Openings. Every Friday evening, from April 24 to October 30 — except in August — the monumental door of the *Pope's museums* will open at sunset to reveal over a thousand years of treasures in the Vatican Collections. The cultural and musical accompaniment to enrich the experience of some of the evening openings has also been confirmed.

As of April 13, 2015, visitors have been able to appreciate the natural and architectural beauty of Vatican City and the Gardens in a new, unprecedented and sustainable way. Comfortably seated on board an environmentally friendly open bus offering panoramic views, with the help of an audio-guide, they will be able to discover the silence and the botanical treasures of the "green heart" of the Vatican along an evocative itinerary bringing together art, nature, and faith. For walking enthusiasts, the traditional guided tour of the Gardens on foot remains available as always! Entrance to the Gardens is denied to persons not properly dressed.

The "Full Day in the Vatican" tour includes a special train that takes people from the Vatican City train station to the Pontifical Villas at Castelgandolfo south of Rome. This was inaugurated

Joan's Rome: Travel Advice

Saturday, September 12, 2015. Offered by the Vatican Museums, this unique tour is offered only on Saturdays and costs just 40 euros for the round trip.

It includes a visit to the Vatican Museums and Vatican Gardens. Those taking the special tour will be given priority entrance to the Vatican Museums, which includes a visit to the Sistine Chapel. After this, participants will spend an hour in the Vatican Gardens. From there, it is a short journey to the Vatican City train station, where passengers will depart for Albano Laziale, about 25 kilometers from Rome. Then passengers will be transferred by shuttlebus to the Pontifical Villas in nearby Castelgandolfo.

At the end of the day, participants will be taken to the San Pietro train station in Rome, which is located near the Vatican. The Pontifical Villas in Castelgandolfo have traditionally served as the Papal summer residence, although Pope Francis has chosen to spend his summers in Rome. Last year, the Vatican Museums began offering tours of the Villas.

The new "Full Day in the Vatican" tour will be the first time the Vatican train station has offered a regularly scheduled passenger train, and audio-guides for the entire tour will be offered in Italian, English, and Spanish. More information can be found on the website of the Vatican Museums.

Audio-guides may be rented at the entrance to the Vatican Museums. For information and reservations, telephone +39.06. 69883229 or +39.06.69881898.

A cafeteria is open during visiting hours.

A note from Joan: For much of the tourist season—which, in Rome, is at least ten months a year—the lines to get into both the museums and the basilica are indescribably long, and the wait can take a great portion of the day you had planned to spend in an altogether different manner. All that changes if you reserve your museum visit in advance: When in Rome, call the numbers that appear above, or fax 06.69885100. You will be given a date and a reservation number (you may also receive these by email or fax if that is how you contact the museums). On the date of your visit, go to the small square at the museum entrance and look for the sign that says "For Reservations Only" or "Reserved Groups." Show you e-mail or fax or state your name and reservation number, and you will then be led into the museums to join your group. I have accompanied friends and relatives who reserved in this fashion and the "thank you" smile on their faces was my best compensation!

Visits to the Roman Necropolis in the Via Triumphalis: The Necropolis can be visited only through prior written bookings. This can be arranged by emailing: visitedidattiche.musei@scv.va.

Now that you have all this information, it would be wonderful if you helped me spread the word! Tell your friends and relatives who will be coming to Rome to *buy this book* and also email the link to this column at *Joan's Rome* to people you know who are planning a trip to Rome and the Vatican.

SO YOU WANT A GREAT MEAL ...

Some advice for a great dining experience: carefully read the menu and know the price of each dish you are ordering. Waiters often make wonderful suggestions, *but* be sure to ask the price of a dish they offer (very especially of fish dishes) or a bottle of wine. You don't want to get an unpleasant surprise when you get the bill; knowing in advance will save time and money.

Joan's Rome: Travel Advice

Italians have a wonderful way of looking at dining, be it at home or in a restaurant. This is a time to share with friends, to enjoy a good meal and great wine, to laugh and talk and relax. They feel bad if you eat hurriedly because, for example, you have to catch a tour, but they rejoice if you linger over dinner for hours. That table is yours for the duration! And, in any decent Italian restaurant, you get your bill only when you ask for it! The restaurant owners I know here are horrified when I tell them that, in the United States, a waiter generally brings your bill before you ask for it!

A tip about tips: Most restaurants add a per person "bread and cover" charge (*pane e coperto*) to the bill, ranging from 1 euro to several euros. Often—but not always—a 12 to 15 percent service charge is added by the establishment. If it has not been added on (check your bill), add it yourself. Check the accuracy of every bill before paying cash or signing for a credit card.

Check the menu to see if there is a cover or service charge. I have seen many a person not leave a tip, as they assumed it was included in the price of the food or service charge—something they never assume in the United States, for example. Ten percent would be a decent minimum tip. By the way, in Italy, when you use a credit card, there is no extra line on the bill to add a tip! Tips, therefore, must be cash.

La Vittoria, Via delle Fornaci 15, Tel. 06.635318: 100 meters south of left-hand colonnade of St. Peter's Square. Take the underground walkway just off the colonnade, and La Vittoria is on your left as you exit the walkway. Ask for Claudio, and tell him Joan sent you. Great food and company and views and reasonable prices. Claudio and his wife, Palmerina, are the welcoming and smiling faces of this restaurant that draws Swiss Guards, Roman Curia personnel, and the staff and seminarians of the North American College. Closed Tuesdays.

LA SCALETTA DEGLI ARTISTI, Via di Santa Maria dell'Anima 56, Piazza Navona area. Tel. 06.68801872; e-mail: info@lascaletta-roma.it. You will always get an amazing meal here and have a great time enjoying it! Ask for Joe, the owner (who speaks six languages, including Arabic), Sali (a superfriendly waiter with seven languages), Alex (who speaks Italian and Portuguese), and then there's Francesco, the Sicilian Bill Murray lookalike chef. Just tell them "Joan sent me!" This is the only place where I dine in the Piazza Navona area.

PIERLUIGI is located on Piazza de Ricci — not far from Piazza Farnese, about a fifteen-minute walk from the Vatican — unbeatable food, fantastic wine list, superb staff. Ask for the owner, Roberto, or his son Lorenzo, and tell them Joan sent you. Fairly expensive but totally worth it, especially for the fish. Try to eat there when the weather is good, and they serve outside on the piazza. Closed Mondays. Tel. 06.6861302.

ZI GAETANA, Via Cola di Rienzo 263, owned by the Cataldi family for the past 80-plus years. The name means "Aunt Gaetana," and four of Gaetana's grandchildren now own and run the place. Innovative menus, good wine list, good prices on the lunch menu.

LO SCARPONE (the name means "boot" or "big shoe"), Via San Pancrazio 15 in Monte Verde neighborhood. Specializes in steaks and grilled meats. Everything here is good. Large outdoor terrace as well as big rooms inside. Frequented by people from Pontifical North American College and by Vatican clergy.

Joan's Rome: Travel Advice

IL FALCHETTO, Via dei Montecatini, 12, off Via del Corso in central Rome. A wonderful menu: Roman dishes and specialties. Rustic and homey atmosphere, fascinating history. Closed Fridays.

L'EAU VIVE, Via Monterone 85. An unusual treat: a French restaurant not far from Piazza Navona run by a lay sisterhood of missionaries from five continents The sisters wear traditional dress, mostly African, and they pray and sometimes dance to prayer at 10 p.m. each evening—usually to the great surprise of diners! Each floor has a different decoration; the ground floor is the most basic, and there is a fairly varied menu, price-wise.

DA GINO, in the Trastevere neighborhood of Rome on Via della Lungaretta. Very good menu: typical regional and local dishes; lots of Roman dishes and some innovative combinations and pretty amazing salads. Dining indoors or outdoors, weather permitting. Closed Wednesdays.

Create your own adventure and find great restaurants on your own!

A note on lodgings in Rome: One area in which I cannot help people—simply because it is too time-consuming—is finding accommodations. If you seek a hotel via the Internet (www.booking.com, TripAdvisor, and so forth), you might also try to search under B&B (bed and breakfast) or even under "Residence." A residence is part hotel (often has a lobby and reception area but no room service and so forth) and part apartment (you have a kitchen and so forth, and it is like being at home, in a way). If large families are traveling or perhaps close friends or relatives, such as two or three couples, this can be a wonderful—and far more economical—way to travel.

A HOLY YEAR IN ROME

You might also want to look at convents. I know many people who have had the vacation of a lifetime by staying at a religious house, whether or not they understood the language! In any event, Italians are famous for communicating with a smile and charade-like gestures! Convents generally have chapels and often have daily Mass. The only drawback might be a curfew, as most convents do have evening deadlines. The Santa Susanna website is extremely helpful in this respect. Check it out at www.santasusanna.org, and go directly to "Coming to Rome."

There are so many categories of hotels, and the ratings here can differ so greatly from ratings of U.S. hotels that a three-star in Rome often does not equal a three-star in the States or in Canada. Always check the U.S. dollar-euro exchange rate when you travel. Sites such as www.booking.com and TripAdvisor.com can be helpful and produce excellent results. However, be sure to do three things once you think you have found the right hotel: (1) visit the hotel's website; (2) read the reviews by past guests, and (3) check the map to be sure it is in the location you want. Good luck and safe travels!

Chapter XII

SANTA SUSANNA, THE AMERICAN AND ENGLISH-SPEAKING CATHOLIC COMMUNITY IN ROME

❖

Alert: As this book goes to press, the church of Santa Susanna has been closed for repairs to the ceiling. The rector, Paulist Father Greg Apparcel, parish lawyers, canon lawyers, and others have been working with Vatican authorities and the Vicariate of Rome to get the church reopened in time for the Jubilee Year of Mercy. Santa Susanna had a full calendar of events for the Jubilee Year 2000, including Masses with U.S. bishops who accompanied pilgrimage groups to Rome, and the parish hopes to have such a calendar for the Jubilee of Mercy.

Please consult the website (www.santasusanna.org), as it will have updates and information on where community Masses will be held in the eventuality that Santa Susanna is not open for the start of the Jubilee on December 8, 2015. Saturday evening Masses at 5:45 are currently held in the Carthusian Chapel of Santa Maria

Maggiore, and Sunday morning Masses are at 9 a.m. at the main altar of this basilica. A Sunday Mass at 10 a.m. is currently being celebrated at San Camillo de Lellis church.

For over three decades I have been a member of Santa Susanna, the Catholic Church in Rome for the English-speaking community. Although the church itself belongs to the Cistercian Sisters, in 1922 it was designated by Pope Benedict XV as the National Church for American Catholics visiting or living in Rome and was entrusted to an American community of priests, the Paulist Fathers.

For decades, this immensely beautiful and historical church in the heart of Rome has been a "home away from home" for a sizable American community, as well as for Australians, Canadians, and British, to name but a few of those who make up our international church family.

The Paulist Fathers perform all the liturgical and other services that one would expect in any parish church: daily and Sunday Masses, confessions, baptisms, weddings, and funerals. The community also comes together many times during the year for social functions: formal dinners, informal potluck meals and fundraisers, and to celebrate important events in our lives as a Church family.

There is a well-run parish council that meets regularly to discuss parish activities and finances, the running of the well-equipped library adjacent to the church, and other parish-related matters. In addition, staff and parishioners participate in civic, religious, and charitable events and organizations in Rome. Every Sunday, following the 10:30 a.m. Mass (the second of two), parish members, guests, and visitors meet for coffee and *cornetti* in the back of the church. Tours of the church are often conducted at this time.

A high point in Santa Susanna's history occurred on June 27, 1993, when, following eight years of restoration of the centuries-old wood ceiling and the reopening of the church after a brief "exile" to St. Agnes in Piazza Navona, Pope John Paul II celebrated Mass there.

Santa Susanna yearly publishes a book entitled *As Romans Do*, which features articles on life in Rome, stories on the Vatican, and biographies of the current U.S. ambassadors (to Italy, to the Holy See, and to the Rome-based FAO, the United Nation's Food and Agricultural Organization), in addition to pages of information about the church itself: address, useful telephone numbers, Mass and Confession times, library hours, background on the Paulist Fathers currently serving, the parish council, and parish activities. This book is free to all visitors, as it is entirely supported by private advertising. It is immensely useful, whether you are in Rome for a week or have come for the rest of your life!

Santa Susanna, just to give you a brief historical overview, is a splendid example of Roman Late Renaissance (also called Mannerism). The church we see today, like most of Rome's old and famous churches, is the result of centuries of building, additions, and restorations.

It was built on the spot that tradition says was the house where Susanna and her father, Gabinus, lived during the reign of the emperor Diocletian (280-290). Susanna and Gabinus, newly converted Christians, had offered their home for the celebration of the Eucharist as early as 285. Both had refused to worship the pagan gods, and, in addition, Susanna had refused a marriage offer from the son of Diocletian. For these reasons they were martyred. They are buried, together with St. Felicity, Pope St. Eleutherius, and St.

Genesius, in the *Confessio* beneath the main altar. This is reached by an elicoidal staircase and is open to visitors.

The floor of the sacristy is partially made of Plexiglas, allowing visitors to gaze down into what remains of the first basilica constructed over Santa Susanna's house at the very end of the sixth century. Beneath these ruins lie what remains of the house of Sts. Susanna and Gabinus.

One of only a handful of churches in Rome entirely decorated in frescoes, Santa Susanna's stunning interior (including the beautiful carved wood ceiling) takes your breath away the moment you enter—if the façade designed by Carlo Maderno and completed in 1603 had not already done so. By the by, Maderno's façade for Santa Susanna's was considered to be so beautiful that he was immediately commissioned to design the façade of St. Peter's Basilica.

While the original sixth-century basilica of Santa Susanna had three naves, the interior today (ordered by Cardinal Jerome Rusticucci, the Pope's vicar and titular of Santa Susanna, who is buried in the crypt) was completed in 1595 and has a single nave, two side chapels (the Chapel of St. Lawrence on the left, and the Chapel of the Crucifix on the right), and an apse. The floor, originally terra-cotta, as in the two side chapels, was redone in 1830 in black, gray, and white marble.

Santa Susanna is the seat of a titular cardinal. In recent decades this has been the cardinal-archbishop of Boston, Massachusetts, USA.

English Mass is also offered Sundays at 10 a.m. at the beautiful and historical church of Santo Spirito in Sassia, on the corner of Via dei Penitenzieri and Borgo Santo Spirito, just minutes from St. Peter's Square. St. John Paul II appointed this church as the Divine Mercy Spirituality Center in Rome in 1994. Santo Spirito (Holy Spirit) is run by the Congregation of Sisters of Our Lady of Mercy.

Santa Susanna

It has a definite link to another Holy Year. There was already a church on this spot in the eighth century that was rebuilt by Pope Sixtus IV for the Jubilee Year of 1475, and again later by Pope Paul III, who commissioned the work to Antonio di Sangallo. The third chapel on the right side is dedicated to Divine Mercy and to St. Faustina Kowalska. The Sunday Mass in English is promoted by the Pontifical Council for Promoting the New Evangelization.

My heartfelt thanks to the Paulist Fathers and to my fellow parishioners at Santa Susanna, whose friendship, affection, understanding, and support has added an incredibly wonderful dimension to my life—and whose input and encouragement made much of this book possible.

Chapter XIII

ODDS AND ENDS: MISCELLANEOUS TIPS FOR TOURISTS

—————————— ❖ ——————————

AMERICAN EMBASSY. There are two official U.S. embassies in Rome: one to the Quirinale or Italian government, and another that represents the United States to the Holy See. Both, as of September 2015, occupy large adjoining but separate premises on Via Veneto and Via Salustriana in the heart of Rome. Americans in need of services must go to the Consulate at 121 Via Veneto (adjacent to the embassy itself). The Consulate can provide the following services: register your address and presence in Italy; issue new passports (I recommend carrying with you—but separate from your actual passport—a photocopy of the first several pages of your passport, as well as those of family members); register your child's birth and give advice about dual citizenship; witness and notarize documents; provide veterans' and social security benefits; process income tax; assist with voting needs and selective service registration; help with legal formalities in case of death; inform your family if you are in difficulty; and provide a list of doctors and lawyers. The Consulate cannot, however, give you money, settle disputes, or get you out of jail. They can only ensure that you are being treated according to the laws of the host country. Telephone: 06.46741.

For other English-speaking citizens, the following embassies are listed in the Rome telephone book:

AUSTRALIA
    Via Antonio Bosio, 5
    Telephone: 06.852721; fax: 06.85272300
    http://www.italy.embassy.gov.au

UNITED KINGDOM
    Via XX Settembre, 80/a
    Telephone: 39.06.42200001; fax: 39.06.42202333
    http://www.britain.it
    Consular assistance: Passports 06.48903708

CANADA
    Via Zara 30, 00198 Rome
(Immigration/Visa and Consular Canadian Citizen Services)
    Telephone: 39.06.854443937
    Via Salaria, 243, 00199 Rome
(Political, Academic, Cultural, and Trade Sections)
    http://www.canadainternational.gc.ca/italy-italie/offices-bureaux/embassy-ambassade.aspx?lang=eng#services

IRELAND
    Embassy of Ireland
    Villa Spada, Via Giacomo Medici 1, 00153 Rome
    Telephone: 39.06.5852381; fax: 39.06.5813336

https://www.dfa.ie/irish-embassy/italy/

NEW ZEALAND
Via Clitunno 44
Telephone: 39.06.8537501; fax: 39.06.4402984
http://www.nzembassy.com/italy

ANTIQUES. Some antiques, regardless of private ownership or foreign origin, are considered part of the patrimony of Italy and may not be exported. So, before you buy that Etruscan vase, find out whether you can take it with you—or whether you will have to return to Rome yearly to visit it!

BARS. In Italy, the word *bar* usually refers not to a cocktail lounge but to a place where you can buy coffee, sandwiches, and other light snacks, and occasionally a hot meal. Wines and spirits are, however, available. Most bars charge different prices at a counter than at a table. Italians, for example, drink their cappuccino and espresso in a few seconds, standing at the counter, whereas tourists enjoy relaxing over coffee, seated at a table. The difference may be more than just that of sitting or standing: tables can entail higher prices, so check the posted price list to see what a coffee or sandwich costs at the counter or at a table. Sitting at a table at an outdoor cafe on a pleasant day in one of Rome's marvelous and beautiful piazzas is, however, usually worth the price.

CHILDREN. If you pace your schedule to accommodate children, you will find that they might enjoy the city as much as you do—and even more if you insert some activities geared to the little ones. Rome has a number of beautiful parks, first among them Villa Borghese, where there is a children's movie theater. The Janiculum

A HOLY YEAR IN ROME

Hill (*Gianicolo*) has a stupendous view of Rome and, on occasion, a marionette show! Rome, of course, has a zoo. In addition, south of Rome's historic center is an area called Exposizione Universale di Roma (EUR), where there is a lovely lake, a large park with trees and benches, and lots of space to play and run in. Some children love to visit the famous *Bocca della Verità*, or Mouth of Truth, at the Church of Santa Maria in Cosmedin, Piazza della Bocca della Verità. The story goes that, if you insert your hand into the "mouth of truth" — and you have been telling the truth — you'll get your hand back, in one piece. If not ...!

CLIMATE. Nothing you can change. Winters can be damp and cold, and summers are hot and humid. But when a Roman day is perfectly beautiful, Rome is the best place in the world to be!

CRIME. Like all big cities, Rome has its share. Some of it is avoidable (don't tempt pickpockets with flashy, expensive jewelry, an open or dangling pocketbook, easily accessible wallets, unlocked cars, and so forth) — and some of it is not (a home broken into even though equipped with six locks, an alarm system, and a pit bull!). After a close brush with a band of gypsy children (whose sleight of hand would stagger David Copperfield), or two Formula One aspirants on a motorcycle, your reflexes set in. Hold on tightly to purses and briefcases, keeping them away from the traffic side of the street. *Never* carry large amounts of cash or valuable documents. Keep your eyes open for suspicious characters on buses, especially on the heavily traveled 64, 62, 46, 492, and a few others that frequent the important tourist spots. Warn someone you think is a potential victim — you too would want such a warning! These warnings are not to scare you — they are to alert you and make you cautious.

Miscellaneous Tips for Tourists

CUSTOMS. We are not speaking of the quaint habits or cultural usages of the country you just visited on vacation, but of the uniformed men at U.S. airports who will take away the homemade sausage and cheeses or even an alligator bag that Aunt Luisa gave you. Many such items are disallowed, so check before you leave the States or with U.S. Customs at the embassy to see what items you may bring back home. This will avoid great disappointment. Several other extra-European countries have similarly strict customs rules.

HORSE CARRIAGES. The *carrozzelle* are a very pleasant and comfortable way to visit Rome—but can be dreadfully expensive. Establish the price and time involved with the driver *before* the trip. Insist that he fulfill his part of the bargain—and you'll do likewise. Same advice for Venetian gondola rides.

PHARMACIES. *Farmacia* are usually open from 9:00 a.m. to 1:00 p.m., and again from 4:00 to 7:30 p.m. but most are open nonstop. They can be recognized by a sign hanging outside that features a green cross (occasionally a red cross) on a white background. At night, and on Sundays and holidays, one pharmacy in each district remains open on a rotating schedule. Italy's highly trained pharmacists can be very helpful in dispensing good advice and often save people from making a trip to a doctor's office.

PRESCRIPTIONS. If you take prescription medicine or wear prescription glasses or contacts, carry at least two copies of these prescriptions with you while you travel: keep one on your person, and another in your hotel room.

TAXIS. Always use the white taxis. *Never* use an unmarked cab—or you'll wonder if he is charging you for a ride or selling you his car!

A HOLY YEAR IN ROME

Taxis in Rome start at a base fee, but supplements can be added for Sunday or holiday travel, for service after 10:00 p.m., and service to or from the airport. These surcharges do not appear on the meter — the meter merely starts at a higher base fee. There is a fixed rate of 48 Euros to and from Fiumicino airport. *Tip*: you might hear men inside the terminal, just outside of baggage-claim area, ask if you want a taxi. Do *not* use these taxi drivers: they are what the Romans and legitimate drivers call *abusivi*. Make a habit of taking the taxi driver's number, usually found on a small metal plaque on the back left door. This can prove invaluable, especially if you ever leave something in a taxi. Taxis are available when the light on top of the car is lit.

WATER IN ROME is pure and safe, including the delicious water at Rome's countless public drinking fountains. *Tip*: the water usually comes out of the bottom part of the spigot, as you would expect. However, if you cover this with your finger, the water then comes out of a hole in the top, arching over for you to drink as in a normal drinking fountain! When in Rome you can drink from the fountains, but when traveling, I advise using bottled water.

BIBLIOGRAPHY

Annuario Pontificio. Vatican City: Vatican Publishing House, 1998-2015.

As Romans Do. Rome: Paulist Fathers of the Church of Santa Susanna, 1998.

Bokenkotter, Thomas. *A Concise History of the Catholic Church*. New York: Doubleday, 1990.

Bedini, D. Balduino, O.Cist. *Le Reliquie della Passione del Signore*. Roma: Basilica S. Croce, 1997.

Brezzi, Paolo. *Storia degli Anni Santi, Da Bonifacio VIII al Giubileo del 2000*. Milan: Ugo Mursia Editore S.p.A., 1997.

Caporilli, Memmo. *St. John Lateran Basilica*. Rome: Euroedit s.r.l.

———. *St. Mary Major Basilica*. Rome: Euroedit s.r.l.

Cerioni, Anna Maria, and Roberto del Signore. *The Basilica of Saint Paul Outside-the-Walls*. Rome: The Pontifical Administration of the Patriarchal Basilica of St. Paul, 1991.

A HOLY YEAR IN ROME

De Toth, Msgr. John Baptist. *The Cathedral of the Pope*. Rome: Capitolo Lateranense, 1995.

Drenkelfort, Heinrich, S.V.D. *The Basilica of the Holy Cross in Jerusalem*. Roma: Scuola Tipografica S. Pio X, 1997.

Esposito, Fr. Pino. *I Giubilei Ieri e Oggi, Storia spirituale-pastorale*. Udine, Edizioni Segno, 1997.

Gugliemi, Carla Faldi. *Roma, Basilica di S. Lorenzo al Verano (fuori le mura)*. Roma.

Impagliazzo, Marco. *Gli Anni Santi nella Storia – 1300-1983*. Vatican City: *L'Osservatore Romano*, 1997.

Jung-Inglessis, E. M. *Das Heilige Jahr in Rom – Geschichte und Gegenwart*. Vatican City: Vatican Publishing House, 1997.

Marrocchi, Mario. *I Giubilei, Origini e prospettive*. Milano: Edizioni San Paolo s.r.l., 1997.

Martino, Fr. Sergio. *La Basilica patriarchale di San Lorenzo Fuori le Mura*. Roma: Tipografia Ugo Detti, 1997.

Pustka, Josef. *Basilica di Santa Maria Maggiore*. Roma: D.EDI.T. s.r.l, 1978.

Serving the Human Family: The Holy See at the Major United Nations Conferences. New York: Permanent Observer Mission of the Holy See to the United Nations, Path to Peace Foundation, 1997.

Stravinskas, Rev. Peter M. J., Ph.D, S.T.L., ed. *Catholic Encyclopedia*. Huntington, IN, USA: Our Sunday Visitor, 1991.

The Vatican and Christian Rome. Vatican City: Vatican Publishing House, 1975.

Bibliography

Venier, Elio. *Gli Anni Santi a Santa Maria Maggiore*. Roma: Istituto Salesiano Pio XI, 1998.

WEBSITES

www.vatican.va: source for Prefecture of the Papal Household, Liturgical Celebrations of the Supreme Pontiff, Basilicas and Chapels, Holy See Press Office.

www.vaticanstate.va: source for Joan's Rome Travel Tips and Information on Visiting the Vatican.

www.im.va: This is the official site of the Jubilee of Mercy whose preparation has been entrusted to the Pontifical Council for Promoting the New Evangelization. Along with Holy See Press Office bulletins, this site was my source for all news documents, speeches, and homilies regarding the announcement of the Jubilee of Mercy, the Bull of Indiction, Pope Francis's Prayer, and official calendar of events.

About the Author

JOAN LEWIS

❖

A native of Oak Park, Illinois, Joan has lived in Rome for more than three decades, during which she has worked for or covered the Vatican as a journalist. Fluent in several languages, Joan has been a member of several high-level Holy See delegations to international conferences, covered numerous papal trips, one papal funeral, one papal resignation, two conclaves, and the canonizations of Sts. John XXIII and John Paul II. She reported on the 2005 conclave when she worked at the Vatican and covered the 2013 conclave as Rome bureau chief for EWTN global Catholic television and radio. You can read her daily column, *Joan's Rome*, watch her on EWTN, and listen to her weekend radio show, *Vatican Insider*.

Called "Rome's Joan" by her many friends in the Roman Curia, she is often a guest on Catholic radio and a guest lecturer in Rome and in the United States. Pope Benedict named her a Dame of St. Sylvester in 2005. She is also a Dame of the Constantinian Order and a Lady of the Order of the Holy Sepulchre.

Sophia Institute

Sophia Institute is a nonprofit institution that seeks to nurture the spiritual, moral, and cultural life of souls and to spread the Gospel of Christ in conformity with the authentic teachings of the Roman Catholic Church.

Sophia Institute Press fulfills this mission by offering translations, reprints, and new publications that afford readers a rich source of the enduring wisdom of mankind.

Sophia Institute also operates two popular online Catholic resources: CrisisMagazine.com and CatholicExchange.com.

Crisis Magazine provides insightful cultural analysis that arms readers with the arguments necessary for navigating the ideological and theological minefields of the day. Catholic Exchange provides world news from a Catholic perspective as well as daily devotionals and articles that will help you to grow in holiness and live a life consistent with the teachings of the Church.

In 2013, Sophia Institute launched Sophia Institute for Teachers to renew and rebuild Catholic culture through service to Catholic education. With the goal of nurturing the spiritual, moral, and cultural life of souls, and an abiding respect for the role and work of teachers, we strive to provide materials and programs that are at once enlightening to the mind and ennobling to the heart; faithful and complete, as well as useful and practical.

Sophia Institute gratefully recognizes the Solidarity Association for preserving and encouraging the growth of our apostolate over the course of many years. Without their generous and timely support, this book would not be in your hands.

www.SophiaInstitute.com
www.CatholicExchange.com
www.CrisisMagazine.com
www.SophiaInstituteforTeachers.org

Sophia Institute Press® is a registered trademark of Sophia Institute.
Sophia Institute is a tax-exempt institution as defined by the
Internal Revenue Code, Section 501(c)(3). Tax I.D. 22-2548708.